THE
RAW TRUTH

SECOND EDITION

THE
RAW TRUTH

Recipes and Resources for the Living Foods Lifestyle

JEREMY A. SAFRON

CELESTIAL ARTS
Berkeley

Published in the United States by Celestial Arts, an imprint of the Crown Publishing Group,
a division of Random House, Inc., New York.
www.crownpublishing.com
www.tenspeed.com

Celestial Arts and the Celestial Arts colophon are registered trademarks of Random House, Inc.

Originally published in the United States in different form by Celestial Arts, Berkeley, California,
in 2003. This new, revised edition incorporates material from *The Raw Foods Resource Guide*,
originally published in 1999 by the Raw Truth Press, Paia, Hawaii, and subsequently revised by
Celestial Arts, Berkeley, California, in 2005. Copyright © 1999, 2005 by Jeremy Safron.

Library of Congress Cataloging-in-Publication Data
Safron, Jeremy, 1971-
  The raw truth : recipes and resources for the living foods lifestyle / Jeremy A. Safron. — 2nd ed.
      p. cm.
  Summary: "Integrates new resources and tips on the raw foods lifestyle into a repackaged edition
of this raw foods recipe book" —Provided by publisher.
  Includes index.
 1. Cooking (Natural foods) 2. Raw foods. I. Title.
  TX741.S24 2011
  641.5'63—dc22

2010035484

ISBN 978-1-58761-040-0

Printed in China

Design by Chloe Rawlins
Front cover food styling by Kim Kissling

10 9 8 7 6 5 4 3 2 1

Second Edition

Contents

Preface to the
Second Edition   vii

Introduction   1

Raw Facts   5

Raw Foods   30

Raw Tools   59

Raw Techniques   64

Recipes   68

DRINKS   69

APPETIZERS   87

FRUIT DISHES   97

FRUIT SOUPS   111

SAVORY SOUPS   117

SALADS   129

DRESSINGS   145

SIDES   153

ENTREES   175

DESSERTS   195

Reading List   209

Glossary   211

Index   212

Preface to the Second Edition

Every journey begins with a single step, yet where it leads depends upon the choices we make along the way. In the past two decades, I've continually evolved my relationship with food in order to eat sustainably, simply, and in harmony with nature while enjoying a diversity of flavors and maintaining a sublime level of health. Sustainable living is more than just electric cars and solar panels. Every item we buy has some impact on the global ecology based on how many resources it takes to get from farm to market. Seventy percent of the world's transportation is used to move or obtain food. People used to farm at home and produce a large amount of their own food. In the 1950s, more than 50 percent of people grew some portion of their food in their backyards. By 1980, less than 5 percent grew their own food and by 2010, it's less than 1 percent. Having a personal interaction with our food helps custom-design the food for our particular needs. A healthy environment grows healthy food, which in turn creates a healthy person.

I remember the first healthy choice I made when I decided to boycott Coca-Cola and rainforest beef during high school. I discovered that my actions had effects on what would be perpetuated in consciousness and sold in the future marketplace. My personal choices in dietary restriction eventually led me to becoming a vegetarian. I put aside meat in order to live a more compassionate and peaceful existence. Soon after, I became a vegan and disposed of all animal products in my life. I fervently read ingredients on every packaged product I consumed or used on my body and I ate only at vegan food establishments. I felt healthy and strong, knowing I was doing my part to make a difference.

I first encountered wheatgrass and some of the basic ideas of raw living foods in 1991. It all made so much sense to me, so I began to incorporate that way of living into my daily life. I started each day with wheatgrass and juices and smoothies. I broadened my palate by seeking out exotic fruits. I would often play in my kitchen, creating recipes based on ones I used to eat and finding a way to make them all raw. I studied some raw foods recipe books and took trips to tropical climates to eat the special fruits that grew there. I began to eat to live rather than live to eat. After more than two years, I was almost 100 percent raw and the only cooked food I ate was the vegan chocolate cake from Angelica's Kitchen in New York City. Knowing that I wanted to be completely raw, I decided to create my own catering company called Loving Foods; I wanted to educate people about raw food and provide delicious meals to show that raw food wasn't just nuts and salad. We launched in Woodstock, New York, in 1993, to great success, and I chose never to eat cooked food again.

I moved to Maui to be the head chef at a retreat center. One night, as I was serving dinner, a few of the local neighbors came by—they would often sneak through the woods to sample the evening meal. The manager of the retreat center said, "There are fifteen people in this workshop and more than twenty people eating dinner here tonight," to which I replied, "I run the kitchen, not the gate, and I'm well within budget." He then said, "These people are here for you; you need a restaurant." I agreed and said, "I do; I quit."

In 1996, I opened the doors of the Raw Experience restaurant in Paia with my partner Renée Loux. We dazzled people with our creative and innovative recipes and the restaurant was a big hit. Yet we always held to our motto of "All Raw, All Vegan, All Organic, All the Time." I wrote the original *Raw Truth* as a book about raw food and the concepts and consciousness that it's based on. But the catering business (which had grown into a restaurant) had many fabulous recipes to share, so I evolved the *Raw Truth* into a recipe book. The original edition was printed at a friend's copy shop and sold out in the first week of printing (there were almost no raw food books available at the time). Soon I took over a friend's shop in San Francisco and the second Raw Experience was opened.

I consulted for other restaurants and began leading my own workshops. I continued to study herbology, natural medicine, farming, permaculture, and exotic fruits and constantly worked to improve my understanding of healthy eating. Sadly, in 1999 we closed the doors of the Raw Experience. I continued teaching and spent a fair bit of time using my body as my laboratory and learning what worked best for me. I would often fast, or live solely on food that I picked myself. Currently I grow much of what I eat, and I include raw dairy in my diet. I recently had the opportunity to work with the University of Hawaii culinary students in a sold-out event. The students and public were awed and delighted by the fantastic five-course meal these culinary students prepared. It is a true pleasure to see raw food cuisine becoming more and more widespread and accepted. I've always found that the most important ingredient in any meal is the love and attention we bring to it. Above all, raw food is about connecting with nature and being ecological, sustainable, and healthy.

Introduction

With the correct tools and the proper resources, we can accomplish anything we wish. Experience (what we do) plus knowledge (what we learn) gives us wisdom (what we can share).

Raw Experience

Experience is the greatest teacher there is. Our lives are our lessons, and contained within them is the information that will allow us to grow. It is up to each of us to decide what our life will hold. Each lesson we learn leads to the next, and as we encourage greater diversity of experience, our ability to comprehend our life lessons increases. The many choices that we make help define how we relate to the world. We change our world as much as our world changes us. The less impact we inflict upon this world, the better we will be able to enjoy it in our future. Reading or hearing about the experiences of others is not the same as experiencing something ourselves. We may understand someone else's experience, but learning from it is a different matter. The more positive our experiences, the more positive we become about our lives. Savor each experience, for they all help to make us what we are.

Raw Knowledge

A fundamental principle of raw foodism is that life promotes life. Food fresh from nature's garden contains a wide range of nutrients and a powerful life force. Raw foodists believe in living as closely to the earth as possible and respecting all life. We suggest growing your own food and trading with other farmers, obtaining it from local farmers' markets, or even foraging for it. We advocate the use of food as medicine, and fasting as a way to cleanse and purify your body and soul. We recognize that if you feed a person a sprout they eat for a day, but if you teach them to sprout, they eat for life and can teach others, too. With the correct tools and the proper resources, we can accomplish anything we choose.

Foods that have been heated or overly processed have lost most (and often all) of their life force. The beneficial enzymes in food are completely destroyed by the heating process, causing the digestive system and body to work much harder to gain any energy or nutrition. If we heated the human body to over 108°F, it would be very uncomfortable, and if we went over 116°F, it would be dead. The same can be said of our foods.

Another tenet of raw foodism is that eating to live is better than living to eat. Most of what is consumed today is overly processed factory farmed consumables. In fact, much of the food eaten today is "edible media;" mainstream society eats for entertainment rather than energy and nutrition. This edible media usually contains little to no nutrition or life force, but it is well packaged and marketed, so people continue to eat it.

Many people have thought they could outsmart nature and profit by isolating the beneficial substances in a food. At first people ate oranges and were healthy. Then someone discovered vitamin C and decided that it was the healthful part of the orange. Later it was realized that ascorbic acid was important for the absorption of vitamin C. Then they figured out that it was the bioflavonoids they needed. Eventually, they will realize that all we needed was the orange all along, and that nature made it perfectly in the first place.

There are many different ideas within the world of raw food. Some people consider raw food to consist only of fruits and leaves, while others suggest dining on elaborate raw recipes made in the tradition of a variety of cultures. There are groups that eat only living food—foods that may have been cooked at one point but have been fully digested by a living culture like miso or nama shoyu. Sproutarians eat mostly sprouts, and fruitarians eat only fruits. My current philosophy is bio-unity—being one with nature and foraging or gardening as much of the food that I eat as possible, and always being creative and loving with my food.

My suggestion for people transitioning to a raw lifestyle is "take the best and leave the rest." Find the raw food philosophy or style that works with your life. Whether it is starting the day raw and going as long as you can, or taking one day a week to eat only raw food, be sure to transition in a comfortable way. Going raw is very easy for some but more challenging for others, just like becoming vegetarian. It is a matter of making a conscious choice to eat from the plant kingdom and then educating yourself properly in order to maintain a high level of health.

Eating involves intent as well as nutrition and life force. When we eat foods made with love, we are inspired; when we eat foods made with sugar, we get upset. The way food is handled and cared for also affects its general energy. Food is sensitive to energy: intent and action either help keep the food pure or corrupt it. Grandma's soup doesn't heal because of the recipe; it's Grandma's love that heals. A romantic dinner isn't romantic because of the ingredients; it's the love that makes it what it is. These examples demonstrate how our intent and thoughts can affect our food. This is true for life as well as food. If we enter into a situation with positive intent, we can do anything, and if we act with negativity, anger, fear, and worry, we just can't seem to do anything right. Remember that your words and thoughts make up your world and that our bodies and lives are a reflection of our mind's experience of itself. We are what we think: positive, loving intentions create positive experiences. Intention is everything.

Raw Origins

All living creatures on the planet, except for humans, eat their food in a raw form. No one has to tell the cow to eat grass or the bear to eat berries—they just do it. As humans have evolved, however, most people have been led away from nature and raw food. In reaction, champions of raw foodism have arisen to carry forth nature's cause.

One of the early and better-known advocates of raw food was Jesus Christ. Christ was a member of a community known as the Essenes. The Essenes lived on sprouts and grasses as well as dehydrated breads. Edmond Bordeaux Szekely expounded upon the Essene teachings by bringing us the Essene Gospel of Peace (a translation from the Dead Sea Scrolls). Another early advocate of eating fresh raw foods was Leonardo da Vinci. Leonardo understood the relationship between eating well and thinking well. Many people have heard that Leonardo was a vegetarian, but not as many know of his writings in which he spoke of the importance of using fresh raw fruits and vegetables as one's primary food source.

More recently, several people have stepped forward to revive and broadcast the message of the benefits of raw food. These revivalists include Dr. Ann Wigmore, who in her lifetime spread knowledge about the importance of sprouts and introduced wheatgrass into the human diet; Paul Bragg, the originator of health food stores and a pioneer of health through proper exercise and nutrition; Norman Walker, who researched the healing benefits of juicing and invented the Norwalk Juicer, a juice press that allows us to get the maximum nutrition and minimum oxidation from our juice and to this day is still arguably the finest juicer available; T. C. Fry, who expounded the teachings of fruitarianism and helped bring about the natural hygiene movement of the 1970s; and Herbert Shelton, whose teachings on fasting and cleansing have inspired so many. All these teachers have brought to light the crucial teachings of eating uncooked foods straight from nature.

More recently, an environmental movement revolving around raw food has emerged. Many people wish to seek out nature, which has been eradicated in many places, to regain their health and their connection with Mother Earth. Just by eating naturally and by producing as little impact on our bodies (and the planet) as possible, each individual can contribute to the raw food movement. Remember, you are what you eat. The tools, techniques, and recipes you'll find on the following pages will give you a solid understanding of raw living. Use the knowledge to inspire or enhance your own raw experience.

Raw Facts

The advantages of eating raw food include everything from benefiting from the live enzymes contained in raw foods to ingesting a greater quantity of vitamins and other vital life-force nutrients. Heat changes the makeup of all things. When food is heated, it is chemically altered and loses most of its ability to provide energy. Eating raw items makes 100 percent of the food's nutrition available to us. According to Dr. Ann Wigmore of the Ann Wigmore Natural Health Institute, the same food in cooked form can have up to 85 percent less nutritional value. Once cooked, many foods combine to form new substances that may be palatable but are by no means beneficial.

Eating living foods also helps us to obtain all of its enzymes, catalysts that help us digest our food. Enzymes remain intact below temperatures of 116°F (and ideally below 108°F); higher temperatures destroy the enzymes and our bodies have to work harder to digest the foods we consume. Enzyme-rich foods help provide our bodies with a more efficient energy source. Raw foods rapidly digest in our stomach and begin to provide energy and nutrition quickly. When you consume cooked food, either alone or before raw food, it can cause a condition called leukocytosis, an increase in white blood cells. Our bodies may respond to cooked food as if it were a foreign bacteria or a diseased cell, which causes our immune system to waste energy on defending us. By eating only raw food or eating raw food before cooked food, you can prevent leukocytosis.

Raw food contains all the enzymes necessary to break itself down, thereby providing you with the maximum amount of energy with minimal bodily effort. Raw food is therefore more wholesome, assimilable, and digestible. Food eaten raw creates very little impact on the body's systems. I also find that raw foods have a far greater range of tastes than cooked foods. Plants take Earth's natural resources and produce a substance that provides energy with no need for alteration. It is truly a gift to be respectful and gentle with the foods that nature provides, in the process benefitting both ourselves and the natural world we live in.

Benefits of Raw Food

A wide range of benefits comes from eating an ideal diet. One of the best advantages of eating raw food is the abundant energy it provides. Energy that is spent digesting cooked food can be made free for us to use for other things when we eat raw. People eating raw foods find that they need to sleep less to feel rested and often attest to achieving life goals that seemed unachievable when on a cooked food diet. Many athletes have found that light raw meals give them a more sustainable form of energy and allow them to surpass their previous records. Students also find that raw food gives them a more balanced blood sugar level and helps them think more clearly and stay more focused. Indigenous people throughout the world demonstrate the great life extension benefits that raw food has to offer. Many of these cultures eat a primarily raw diet and live much longer lives. People eating raw food also find it enhances their beauty. Most of all, people who eat well feel good. Feeling good is the essence of life. We enjoy our lives more when we feel good. The Hawaiians say that the most valuable thing a person can have is a positive attitude. By eating well and feeling good, we can be more positive and create a better life for ourselves and those we love.

A Plant's Intention

A plant's intention is to grow. It sprouts from a seed and produces and uses chlorophyll to combine sunlight and carbon dioxide with other nutrients found in soil to create more of itself. As more and more leaves are produced, a plant matures enough to bear fruit. Plants take the elemental minerals in soil (in their raw form), absorb them, and transform them into organic minerals that animals can assimilate. Plants are not harmed when their fruit is eaten. It actually benefits the plant. The fruit's intention is to be eaten so that its seeds can spread to other places to further propagate the species. To enable this process, fruit looks and tastes delicious. It many ways, all creatures who eat fruit are giving life to future generations of fruit, as well as absorbing nutrients. Some plants continually produce fruit, while others produce fruit once and pass back into the earth. Plant a seed and create a future meal. As we sow, so shall we reap.

Preprogrammed versus Processed

In today's world, commercially produced foods are grown with an agenda. First, a seed is planted, usually not with the intention to forward life, but rather to benefit the farmer financially. Then, as the seeds grow into plants, they are often treated with toxic chemicals (under the guise of protecting the plant and us from bugs). After that, the plants are either harvested by fossil fuel–burning machines or by poorly paid, disgruntled workers. The fruit and vegetables produced from these plants are then shipped, usually many miles, before being tossed around by workers who care nothing for the produce.

Often the next step is that an underpaid produce clerk puts the fruits and vegetables on a shelf, where they are sprayed with chlorinated water after they have been coated with an animal-based wax. This produce is often made to look homogeneous, and it tastes like a synthetic version of the real thing. In the store, the fruits and vegetables sit under fluorescent lights until someone buys them and takes them home. Sometimes the produce is sent to factories, where machines with grease and dirt flying about mash, mutilate, cook, and kill every possible raw nutrient and all the food's life force. Then the fruits and vegetables are packaged and sent to a supermarket near you, where they sit on the shelf indefinitely. By the time you buy the box or can containing the fruits and vegetables, there may be more nutritional value in the package than in the product inside.

From the Tree Right to Me

Conversely, there are still some farmers who refuse to participate in the mass mechanization and chemicalization of the food industry. They grow their food without chemicals or pesticides and still harvest by hand. This food is referred to as "organic" or "unsprayed" and, from a nutritional and energetic point of view it is the best store-bought food to consume. There are many alternatives to shopping at a grocery store. Local farmers' markets, farmstands, co-ops, and natural food stores offer an abundance of consciously raised, organic, unsprayed, and locally grown food. Homegrown foods and those harvested from the wild are the best available. Only nature and the forager are involved in creating a direct connection between the earth and human. Growing your own food in a greenhouse or garden is a way to ensure that love goes into the growth of a plant. When we interact with our food in a positive way, the food provides far more energy. Positive interaction with plants can increase the plant's yield and vitality.

Enzymes

Live enzymes are essential to digestion. Enzymes break down the food we eat into a usable form for the body. When a food is exposed to temperatures greater than 116°F (or, to a lesser extent, anything above 108°F), most of its enzymes are killed. Enzyme-depleted food can be very hard to digest and provides the body with very little energy. Without the valuable enzymes contained in raw and living food, our body must produce some of its own enzymes to digest food. This process leaves the body drained of energy. Raw and living food can fill the body with energy and vibrancy rapidly by breaking down food quickly for easy digestion and assimilation. Since many nuts and seeds contain a coating of enzyme inhibitors that stop the digestive breakdown of the seed, seeds should be soaked in water or sprouted so they become digestible, alive, and packed with nutrients.

Assimilation and Elimination

Illness and disease are symptoms of either poor assimilation or poor elimination. For many reasons, from a deficient diet to poor lifestyle choices, the body can become filled with toxic matter that poisons the body, mind, and spirit. This toxic matter sometimes clogs the body and greatly reduces the ability of the body to absorb nutrients. The body then becomes starved of valuable vitamins, minerals, and amino acids that keep the body functioning optimally. This is known as poor assimilation.

When toxic or harmful substances are taken into the body but cannot be moved out of the body, it is called poor elimination. Organic raw and living foods benefit both assimilation and elimination, helping to keep the body free from illness. The foods many people have consumed earlier in life have often been less than healing for their bodies, and this can result in a clogged colon. The colon is where we get most of the nutrition out of our foods. At present, many people have their colons clogged with fecal mucoid matter. This debris can sometimes cover the majority of the surface area of the intestinal walls. The walls of the intestines are covered with many folds, curves, and fingerlike projections called villi, which are designed to take in nutrition. When the colon gets overly impacted with fecal mucoid matter, our ability to take in nutrition is degraded.

Many people eat a lot and yet are unable to get what their body needs. In fact, some of the best-fed people in the world suffer from malnutrition. A contributing factor to effective assimilation is healthy intestinal flora. Eating food in the correct combinations and chewing well also improve assimilation. Fresh raw juice and fruits are the easiest to assimilate. Greens and fibrous foods are wonderful for cleaning out the intestines of old debris. Eating raw food allows for the maximum assimilation of what food has to offer. Many of our true food cravings are nutritionally based. Our bodies know what they need and send word to our senses to seek out foods with these nutrients. In order to absorb the nutrients we seek, we need to have healthy assimilation. If not, we will eat much greater amounts of food in an attempt to get the nutrients we need. Raw food, with all of its nutrients and enzymes intact, is very easy to absorb and often helps cleanse the body and promote greater assimilation.

Elimination is the process of removing from the body something that is useless or toxic. Many people pick up bacteria or toxic food substances and become ill. This is because their bodies are not releasing the harmful substances. When a healthy body encounters toxic materials, it will quickly pass them out of the system. When toxic materials are encountered by a body suffering from poor elimination, they may get stuck in the system and cause disease. Toxic debris can build up in the body for many years and eventually cause health issues. By eliminating potentially harmful substances from our diet, we protect our body and promote greater health and longevity.

Organically Distilled Water

Water is one of the fundamental elements of life, and humans are composed of almost 80 percent water. Finding pure sources of water is of the utmost importance in this modern era, when environmental toxins abound. In ancient times, the purest water came from wells, streams, and rainwater. Now, a hundred years after the introduction of chemicals and pesticides, well water, rivers, and rain are often polluted. Tap water is even worse, as it has usually been treated with "cleansing" chemicals. Additionally, tap water and bottled water often go through plastic pipes (a synthetic material, neither organic or inorganic). There are various methods of obtaining pure water through mechanical or natural means—such as evaporation or filtration—but the best source of all is directly from plants.

Plants have the natural ability to distill water. A tree will draw inorganic minerals into its roots from stream runoff, rain, and underground springs and transform it into organically distilled water that it will store in its leaves and fruits. This organically distilled water held in the plant's living cells can be obtained by juicing or eating watery fruits or by drinking coconut water. The method by which modern water purifiers remove unwanted chemicals and bacteria is very similar to that of a plant. Filters range from those that eliminate only odors and tastes to those that remove all unwanted inorganic minerals and harmful bacteria. Many people in the natural hygiene tradition use water distillers, which evaporate the water and recondense it, leaving any toxic sediment behind. There are also companies that sell bottled water that is especially pure and water that has been ozonated or oxygenated.

Both filtered water and organically distilled water can be further improved through a restructuring process that results in what's referred to as *charged water*. To make charged water, pour purified or clean water (water that doesn't need to be filtered or purified, such as fresh spring water or well water) back and forth three to seven times between two glass jars, then leave it to settle in one of the jars. Add a quartz crystal to the water, then put the water in direct sunlight for twenty-four hours or more. The resulting water will be recharged and holistically structured.

The Four Living Food Groups

The four primary categories of living foods are fresh food, sprouted food, cultured food, and dehydrated food. Fresh food is any type of raw food that is ready for use in its vibrant unadulterated form. Examples of fresh foods are fruits, vegetables, fresh herbs, and other harvested food. Fresh foods represent the element of Water and are life giving.

Sprouted food is any type of seed, nut, grain, or bean that has been soaked in water, exposed to air and indirect sunlight, and, when rinsed daily, forms a new plant, beginning with a sprout. Some examples are almond sprouts, buckwheat sprouts, sunflower sprouts, and mung bean sprouts. Sprouted foods represent the element of Air and are regenerating and cleansing.

Cultured food is any type of food that has had a beneficial culture introduced into it (acidophilus, koji, and bifidus, for example). These cultures then grow and proliferate within the food. Some examples are miso, amazake, seed cheeze, kimchee, and tofu. Cultured foods represent the element of Fire and are energizing and transformational.

Dehydrated foods are those from which the water has been removed through gentle drying at low heat. Some examples are dried fruits, Essene bread, and dried herbs. Dehydrated foods represent the element of Earth and are very grounding and sustaining.

Eating 100 percent raw food is easy. It does, however, require eating a balanced diet and a certain understanding about the foods you consume. It's very important to know about foods' nutritional value and what our bodies need in order to make sure these requirements are met. The chart on page 13 gives general guidelines about what makes a well-balanced raw food diet. By increasing the quantity of fresh foods in a cooked diet, the cleansing process begins and helps flush out old toxins and the addictions that go with them. Greens and fresh fruits are especially helpful in pushing harmful debris out of the cells and the colon. These two primary raw food sources allow a person in transition to adjust his body to eating more and more raw food. As a person feels fuller and more nourished from eating raw foods, he may begin to experiment with letting go of cooked food. The cultured foods will really help initiate this by increasing the amount of assimilation through proper intestinal flora. Dehydrated foods will also assist a person craving for something heavy. The chart on page 13 shows an ideally balanced raw food diet that can be continued throughout one's life.

Transitioning Strategies

Each person is unique, and so is her way of eating. In order to transform to a raw plant-based diet, some people may need only a short time, while others may require years to comfortably make the transition. People who were raised on a standard American starch- and meat-based diet may take up to three years to properly transition to a 100 percent living foods diet. Through fasting and cleansing practices, the body can be rebuilt. The cleaner and healthier the body is, the quicker and easier the transition. The four living food groups chart on page 13 can help structure a transition that is easy and healthy. When moving toward healthier eating, it is helpful to work in conscious steps and to stay within your comfort zone. Senseless struggle and self-judgment only impede growth. Dehydrated foods are the closest to cooked foods and can help people who are used to eating bread and pasta. Refer to the following information for the proper percentages that can support transition.

Transitioning Tips

Change is the only constant. In our eternal growth, we often seek out new ways of thinking, living, and even eating. The transitory period between one way and another can be smooth and easy or quite rough and challenging. The following are a few tips on transitioning to raw food, although many can be applied to almost any aspect of your life.

- **Take your time and be patient.** Accentuate the positive. Be focused on the good things you ate and did today. Eat the raw and natural foods you enjoy.

- **Start the day raw and see how far you go.** Drink a smoothie for breakfast, eat salad for lunch, and start your dinner with a raw soup or salad.

- **Have a raw food dinner party or potluck at your home.** It's a great way to try new dishes, turn people on, and support your new lifestyle.

- **Eat one new raw food each day.** Find out what foods you like and don't. Discover the variety of delicious flavors nature has to offer. If you know your foods, you can create any dish.

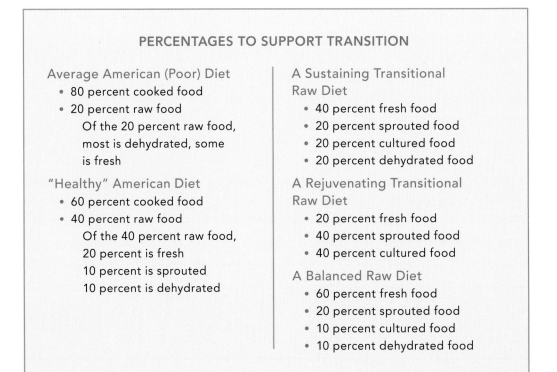

PERCENTAGES TO SUPPORT TRANSITION

Average American (Poor) Diet
- 80 percent cooked food
- 20 percent raw food
    Of the 20 percent raw food, most is dehydrated, some is fresh

"Healthy" American Diet
- 60 percent cooked food
- 40 percent raw food
    Of the 40 percent raw food, 20 percent is fresh 10 percent is sprouted 10 percent is dehydrated

A Sustaining Transitional Raw Diet
- 40 percent fresh food
- 20 percent sprouted food
- 20 percent cultured food
- 20 percent dehydrated food

A Rejuvenating Transitional Raw Diet
- 20 percent fresh food
- 40 percent sprouted food
- 40 percent cultured food

A Balanced Raw Diet
- 60 percent fresh food
- 20 percent sprouted food
- 10 percent cultured food
- 10 percent dehydrated food

- **Go on local plant walks** and familiarize yourself with herbs, fruits, flowers, and greens that grow wild near your home.

- **Dine out at raw cafes** and then go home and re-create your favorite dishes. It is also fun to make old cooked favorites as raw dishes.

- **Always make the best choice.** Eat the thing with the most life force and the foods you know will help you.

- **Know yourself and educate yourself.** Knowledge is power.

FOUR LIVING FOOD GROUPS

10 PERCENT CULTURED FOODS

10 PERCENT DEHYDRATED FOODS

Miso
Live tofu   Oils
Kimchee   Nuts
Rejuvelac   Yeast
Raw vinegar   Sea salt
Sauerkraut   Spirulina
Seed cheeze   Sea vegetables
Seed yogurt   Sun-dried bread
Cultured vegetables   Dried fruits and herbs

20 PERCENT SPROUTED FOODS*

Alfalfa Clover Wheat Corn Oat Rye
Wild rice Millet Quince Amaranth Onion
Garlic Pumpkin Barley Almond Sesame
Sunflower Garbanzo Soy Lentil Pea Hazelnut

All seeds, nuts, and beans are sproutable; some grow sprouts, some grow greens, and some grow grasses.

60 PERCENT FRESH FOODS*

Juicy fruits Berries Sweet fruits Fresh nuts Juices
Flowers Nightshades Greens Wild herbs Roots
Mushrooms Allium Brassica Cucurbits

Unheated (raw) organic foods from nature.

BIO-DESTRUCTIVE TO BIO-GENIC FOODS

Bio-Destructive
(food that is hurtful)

Bio-destructive foods damage and destroy the body's organs and cells and deplete the body's ability to heal itself. These foods are toxic.

Food containing chemicals, preservatives, synthetic materials, artificial colors and flavors, food cooked in aluminum, hormone-raised animal products

Bio-Degenerative
(food that is harmful)

Bio-degenerative foods have a destructive effect over time. They weaken the body and can eventually cause disease.

Meats
Overcooked and packaged food
Old and rotting food
Canned food
Food containing inorganic
   materials
Processed food
Food cooked in oils
Foods frozen for too long
Homogenized and industrially
   processed dairy products
Food containing unknown and
   unpronounceable substances
Food made with anger

Bio-Static (food that is inert)

Bio-static foods require time and energy to digest, giving very little (if anything at all) back to the body. These foods may slightly sustain life.

Cooked fruits
Cooked vegetables
Cooked grains
Cooked beans
Frozen food
Food dried at high temperatures

Bio-Active (food that is helpful)

Bio-active foods have many vital nutrients and allow the body to function optimally. These foods build and maintain the body's normal processes.

Raw, live, organic food
Whole food
Amino-rich food
Enzyme-rich food
Food dried at low temperatures

Bio-Regenerative or Bio-Genic
(food that heals)

Bio-genic foods repair the body and promote longevity and healing.

Rejuvenating food
Sprouts and chlorophyll-rich food
Cultured food
Medicinal herbs
Fresh, wild, hand-picked food
Food made with love

Fresh Foods

It is very important to consume large amounts of fresh foods, such as fruits, vegetables, herbs, and other harvested foods, which should make up about 60 percent of your daily intake. Fresh foods contain a large quantity of organically distilled water (up to 85 percent) and also contain many vital nutrients and vitamins. There is a wide variety of fresh foods, but it is often best to eat fresh foods grown in your own area.

Why Organic?

Organic foods are grown without any chemicals, pesticides, or fungicides. Nonorganic or conventionally grown foods may contain deadly poisons that can cause cell damage and toxic buildup and eventually lead to death. These synthetic poisons are completely foreign to humans and animals, and we are just now beginning to see their effects in civilization. Most farms grow sprayed foods because the spray keeps the pests away, thereby ensuring a larger crop even though the food is deadly. Organic foods are grown the way nature intended, fertilized only with compost made from other organic foods or sea vegetables or plant matter. Plants grown only with these fertilizers are considered grown in a vegan manner (with no animal products). Other organic farming methods entail fertilizing crops with manure and fish emulsion: these are considered organic only if the animals were fed organically.

Seasons of Fruit

Throughout the year, most fruits transition from a fruiting stage, to a dormant stage, to a leaf- and branch-growing stage, to a flowering stage, and then back again to fruiting. Each variety of fruit has its own cycle; some trees fruit in the summer, while others fruit in the spring or fall. Some trees fruit at different times based on their elevation or where, exactly, they are grown. For more information, contact your local farmers to learn what fruits are in season where you live, and start keeping a local seasonal calendar.

Food Combining

Some foods go together quite well, such as mango and papaya, while others don't, like onions and persimmons. For the most part, food combining is intuitive; we do what feels best for our bodies. Some combinations may work wonderfully for one person and not as well for another. There are many philosophies about food combining; some teachings suggest that it is best to eat fruits separately from vegetables. Some even advise eating each type of food alone. The primary reasoning behind these ideas is that different foods take different amounts of time to digest and some can even impede the digestion of other foods.

Foods are often divided into groups such as acid, subacid, and sweet fruits; grains; greens; and other veggies. People who practice proper food combining try to eat only foods that are classified in the same group at the same time. It has been said that fruits, if eaten alone, take only thirty minutes to digest, whereas most other foods take up to seven hours to digest. For this reason, melons are best eaten alone. Melons will be absorbed into the body in fifteen minutes if eaten by themselves, but if eaten in combination with something else, they may take as long as the other food eaten to be digested. The best sign as to whether you are properly combining foods it to look at the quality of stool produced and the sensation the foods give to your body. When foods are eaten in a proper combination, you will feel good and produce no flatulence, and your stool will be solid and not contain any undigested food particles. Creative digestion is the practice of eating what feels good because the body always knows best.

Juicing

Juicing is extracting the organic water from fruits and vegetables, which concentrates the vitamins and minerals by removing the pulp and fiber. Juicing is a great way to stay hydrated and enjoy a wide range of nutrition. Juicing is extremely cleansing and healing.

Fresh Is Best

There is great beauty in consuming foods right under the tree they grew from. Much of the food that is widely available to us is shipped all across the world and stored for extended periods of time. Food, when attached to its root or plant, is still in the process of growing. When we harvest it, it holds its life force for only a short time and then begins to decompose. The closer you are to the source of the harvest, the better the quality of food and the more vital it is. There are a variety of ways to get closer to the source of the food you eat. One way is to contact local farmers in your area. Another way of obtaining fresh foods is to go to a local farmers' market. Of course, the easiest way is to grow your own. Food that we coparent is of the greatest value because it comes imbued with our own energy. Interaction with the plants we eat can heal us and help us grow. Remember, you are what you eat!

Easy Indoor Gardening

Many plants grow easily indoors. Indoor gardening can be crucial for city survival or just to supplement your winter diet with fresh home-grown foods. Sprouts are the most nutritious and most rapidly growing of any indoor-grown food. For instructions on sprouting, see pages 20–23. However, it's easy to grow some fresh foods indoors, too. Beet tops can grow beet greens, and celery bottoms will grow leaves. Beets and other greens can be grown easily by placing the top of the beet or the bottom of a celery stalk in a shallow tray or dish of water. After a few days, the greens begin to grow and can be harvested for many weeks. Herbs such as basil and parsley can be grown indoors year-round. Just provide a bit of light and nourishing soil plus an ample dose of water and you will have a beautiful array of herbs. Even hot pepper plants and edible flowers can be grown indoors easily.

Indoor growing systems are also a good way to grow vegetable and small fruit crops as well as an abundant supply of herbs. Hydroponic (water-grown) or traditional soil-grown plants can be grown indoors. This may require supplemental lighting (fluorescent, halide, or sodium) in order to get a substantial yield. There are many books and guides to growing everything from tomatoes to strawberries in a basement or warehouse. Greenhouses and solariums are some of the best ways to grow your own food year-round.

Cutting and Storing Fresh Foods

When we bite or cut into a fresh food, we rupture its auric field. We are essentially breaking the food's safety seal, which is made up of all the cells of the food. When we slice or puncture these cells, we open up the fruit and allow it to begin to oxidize. Oxidation is the process by which oxygen combines with other available minerals and feeds bacteria so the fruit can go back to the soil and nourish the seeds within it. All of us have experienced biting into an apple, setting it down for a few moments, and seeing it turn brown; that's oxidation. This is one reason that the best method for extracting juice from a fruit or vegetable is to press it. By pressing, we cause cells to rupture from within rather than cutting or popping the cells from the outside. Pressed juice takes up to twenty-four hours to oxidize, while any masticated or centrifugally made juices oxidize in less than an hour. The way we store foods is also important. The ancient Egyptians stored food in pyramids. This allowed grains and seeds to be stored for considerably longer periods of time. The kamut found in King Tut's tomb thousands of years later was still viable and sprouted. Temperature and light play major roles in the storage of foods. Warmth and direct light make food break down more quickly. So keep your fruits dry, cool, and out of the sun.

Sprouted Foods

Sprouted foods, such as almond sprouts, buckwheat sprouts, sunflower sprouts, and mung bean sprouts, are often very high in chlorophyll. In many plants, the highest levels of chlorophyll exist while the plant is in its youngest and most vital stages. Sprouted food is very helpful in the building of new cells, provides existing cells with additional oxygen, and helps rejuvenate the body.

Plants know that their seeds or seed-laden fruits will be eaten—in fact, they plan for it. All seeds, nuts, beans, and grains are coated with an enzyme inhibitor. This inhibitor is designed to protect a seed from the digestive system of animals. When eaten whole and raw, seeds can pass through an animal's digestive system in their entirety and be planted in a pile of fertilizer to grow a new plant. The best way to release the enzyme inhibitor is to sprout the seed or to grind it into a powder. When we grind a seed, we are able to digest it, primarily because we have created a greater surface area and broken through the skin coated with an enzyme inhibitor. Chewing well is a great way to grind seeds. Sprouting, however, completely releases the enzyme inhibitor and also activates the seeds. Soaking a seed for fifteen minutes releases up to 50 percent of the enzyme inhibitors. The recommended soaking times listed in the chart on page 22 are the times required for the maximum release of enzyme inhibitors.

The Benefit of Sprouts

Sprouts are potential energy unleashed. The sprout is the youngest growth of a seed or nut, when the enzyme inhibitors have been released and the food has become enzyme rich. Sprouts, which are quite diverse, are abundant in chlorophyll, a very rich source of protein, and a high-energy food providing a wide range of nutrients.

Sprouted seeds also have more nutrition than their dry predecessors. Some types of sprouts have as much as five times their original nutritional value. A sprout is the baby plant, so it puts an enormous amount of energy into getting those first few leaves out. The sprouting cycle of a plant's life is where it has the most concentrated nutrition. This is because the sprout wants to become a plant and it knows that it must get a root in the ground and a leaf up to the sky. Once rooted, survival will be much easier. Much like all creatures, sprouts go through their most rapid development at this early stage. The equivalent in humans would be learning to walk or talk; for a sprout, it is creating a wide range of enzymes and vitamins and minerals to get a good start in life. The young sprouts and grasses contain the highest amount of chlorophyll that the plant will ever attain. Sprouts are very nutritious and have many rejuvenating benefits.

Chlorophyll

Chlorophyll is liquid life. All plant life is based upon it. Plants use chlorophyll to transform sunlight and CO_2 into sugar and oxygen. The chlorophyll cell and the human red blood cell are molecularly almost identical.

When ingested, chlorophyll is almost instantly absorbed into the body and feeds abundant amounts of oxygen to the blood, brain, organs, and all cells, allowing them to function at an optimal level. It creates an unfriendly environment for harmful bacteria, helping to protect the body from viruses and infections. Chlorophyll helps build the immune system, detoxifies the organs and cells of the body, cleanses the liver of accumulated toxic oils, and aids in healing wounds. Chlorophyll helps protect cells from the harmful effects of radiation from electricity substations, televisions, computers, X-rays, nuclear power plants, and nuclear waste.

Chlorophyll can be found in all green plants, and some plants, such as wheatgrass, contain as much as 70 percent chlorophyll. Sprouting seeds releases the enzyme inhibitors and begins the production of chlorophyll using light and water to create life. Chlorophyll-rich food is full of vital enzymes and essential vitamins. It increases cell growth and thereby helps the body regenerate. Young grasses and sprouts are some of the best sources of chlorophyll, but temperatures greater than 108°F begin to break down the chlorophyll in plants. The higher the temperature, the more quickly the chlorophyll is destroyed, so chlorophyll-rich foods should be eaten raw and not cooked.

Growing Wheatgrass

The young shoots of the wheat plant are a great source of energy and nutrition. Wheatgrass is a power food and provides every vitamin and mineral necessary for human survival as well as helps to reduce radiation poisoning and remove other toxins from the body. Wheatgrass is protein packed, and one ounce of wheatgrass is equal nutritionally to four and a half pounds of vegetables.

Wheatgrass is fun and easy to grow. To sprout wheat, just follow the directions for sprouting seeds (see below), and then spread a thick layer of wheat sprouts on the surface of a tray filled with soil 1$^1/_2$ inches deep, or spread the sprouts on the ground. Then, cover the sprouts with a thin layer of soil. Next, cover the tray with mesh or another tray. Water the wheatgrass every day to keep it moist and after 3 days it will push up the top tray. Remove the tray and continue to water as needed. When the grass is about 5 inches tall, expose it to some sunlight for a few hours each day to help enrich the chlorophyll. Wheatgrass is one of the best sources of this substance, since it contains as much as 70 percent chlorophyll.

There are many varieties of wheat, and all have different purposes. Winter wheat is better for wheatgrass, soft spring wheat is best for fermenting, and summer wheat is nice for dehydration and cereal.

How to Sprout

Sprouting is the easiest way to grow foods for yourself. You can grow sprouts in any climate anywhere in the world. If you can live there, so can sprouts. To sprout, first select the type of seed you wish to grow and refer to the chart on pages 22–23 to find out the optimal soaking time. You can sprout seeds in just about any container, including a cloth bag or even a wicker basket, although a large glass jar ($^1/_2$ to 1 gallon) with a screen cover is the most popular setup. As a general rule, for a yield of $^1/_2$ gallon of sprouted seeds, use 2 to 3 tablespoons of small seeds such as alfalfa or clover; 1$^1/_2$ cups of medium seeds such as wheat, oat, or garbanzo; or 2 to 3 cups of nuts and rice. After soaking them for the appropriate amount of time, drain them and then rinse the sprouts with fresh water at least twice a day until the tails are at least three times the size of the seed in length. Next, expose your sprouts, still in the jar, to sunlight for about 15 minutes to activate the abundance of chlorophyll. Now, chow down!

Sprouting Tips

- If using a jar, it is important to set the jar at a 45-degree angle. This promotes the maximum amount of drainage and an ideal amount of airflow. The easiest way to do this is by placing it in a dish-draining rack or setting it in the sink with a mug or cup to prop it up, or even sticking it leaning against the edge inside a heavy bowl so that it has proper drainage. If using a basket, fill the base of the basket and soak it in a bowl of water. Keep the basket covered with cheesecloth or silk screen and set it somewhere cool and out of sunlight (though not in total darkness). If using a bag, place the proper amount of seeds in the bag and soak in water overnight. Hang the bag above the sink so it can drip and have maximum airflow.

- Make sure that the sprouts can breathe—use wide-mouth jars whenever possible. To cover a sprouting jar, use mesh window screens, or, in a pinch, you can use cheesecloth or even an old T-shirt. There are also sprouting jar lids available commercially.

- Sprouts can drown! Don't soak them for too long.

- Buckwheat and sunflower sprouts are best when planted like wheatgrass in soil and grown into tasty greens.

- Always rinse with filtered water to promote clean sprouts.

Live Cultured Foods

Cultured foods, such as miso, amazake, seed cheeze, kimchee, and tofu, help to promote healthy bacteria within the digestive system. These "friendly" bacteria help break down our food and hand us the vital nutrients that we need. A high concentration of good bacteria allows for maximum absorption and faster assimilation of our food's nutrients. A strong concentration of friendly bacteria will also maintain a healthy balance within the intestines and will not leave room for unfriendly bacteria to grow.

SEED SOAKING AND SPROUTING TIMES

Type of Seed	Amount	Soak Time	Sprout Time* (comments)
Adzuki	1¹/₂ cups	8 hours	3 days
Alfalfa	3 tablespoons	6 hours	3 days
Almond	3 cups	8 hours	1 to 2 days
Barley	2¹/₂ cups	7 hours	2 to 3 days (plant in soil for grass)
Buckwheat, in hull	2 cups	6 hours	2 days (plant in soil for greens)
Buckwheat, no hull	2 cups	10 hours	1 day
Cabbage	3 tablespoons	6 hours	1 day
Caraway	1 cup	6 to 10 hours	1 to 2 days
Cashew	3 cups	5 hours	1 day
Chia	3 tablespoons	6 hours	2 to 3 days
Corn	2 cups	8 to 10 hours	3 days
Cumin	1 cup	7 to 9 hours	1 day
Dill	3 tablespoons	5 hours	2 days
Fenugreek	¹/₂ cup	7 hours	3 days
Flax	3 cups	6 hours	2 to 3 days (1 hour is okay)
Garbanzo	1¹/₂ cups	8 hours	2 to 3 days
Hazelnut	2 cups	8 hours	2 to 3 days
Kamut	2 cups	7 hours	2 to 3 days (plant in soil for grass)
Lentil	2 cups	7 hours	3 days
Macadamia	3 cups	5 to 7 hours	4 days

Type of Seed	Amount	Soak Time	Sprout Time* (comments)
Millet	2 cups	8 hours	3 days
Mung bean	2 cups	8 hours	3 days
Mustard	3 tablespoons	6 hours	2 days
Oat groats	2½ cups	6 hours	2 days
Peanut	2 cups	8 hours	2 days
Peas	2 cups	7 hours	3 days
Pecan	2½ cups	4 hours	1 day
Quinoa	2 cups	6 hours	1 day
Radish	3 tablespoons	6 hours	3 days
Red clover	3 tablespoons	6 hours	3 days
Rye	2 cups	8 hours	3 days (plant in soil for grass)
Sesame	2 cups	6 hours	2 days
Soy	2 cups	8 hours	3 days (1 day for tofu)
Sunflower	3 cups	7 hours	2 days (plant in soil for grass)
Triticale	2 cups	6 hours	3 days
Walnut	2½ cups	4 hours	1 day
Wheat (wheat berries)	2 cups	7 hours	2 to 3 days (plant in soil for grass)
Wild rice	3 cups	9 hours	3 to 5 days

* Sprout time is the time between draining the seeds and eating them. The length of sprouting time may vary based on the climate. These instructions are for a ½-gallon jar or bag.

Culturing

Culturing is the process of encouraging the production of beneficial bacteria in food. Bacteria, such as acidophilus and those found in foods like koji and miso, are all very helpful in the body's assimilation of food. Friendly bacteria live in the digestive tract and break down food so that it can feed our bodies. There are also harmful cultures that can get inside the body and the best way to get rid of them is to have an abundance of good bacteria. Foods such as sprouted beans, nuts, and seeds all culture very well when introduced to bacteria and kept in a warm place. Many cultured products can be made easily, such as kimchee, seed cheeze, rejuvelac, and tofu.

Fermented foods are living foods. A living food is one with live bacteria flourishing in it and that contains organisms that can live in the body of an animal in a symbiotic relationship. It is possible to cook a food and then culture it, but raw foodists believe in sprouting foods to ferment them. It is good to check with local stores to determine how the foods you purchase were shipped and stored, because cultured foods aren't viable once they are frozen or heated. Some foods culture in hours and others in days. Some foods, such as miso and shoyu, can be cultured for years.

What Are Cultured Foods?

Cultured foods are those that have been predigested by a helpful bacteria such as acidophilus, bifidus, or koji. These live cultures reside on the villi, small fingerlike projections that extend from the intestinal walls. The greater the surface area of the villi, the more room there is for healthy cultures to live there. The helpful bacteria that reside in our bodies originally got there through our mother's milk (if we were breast-fed). Cultured foods are live foods. Some cultured foods may have lived on a cooked product. These foods, such as miso, contain none of the original cooked food, only the live raw culture (unless they are pasteurized, in which case the culture is cooked). Many cultured foods live on raw food and are considered both raw and live. These are the ideal cultured foods. Some great-tasting cultures are even grown on sprouts.

What Do Cultured Foods Do for Us?

Cultured foods both protect us from foreign bacteria and energize us through proper assimilation. These helpful bacteria, such as acidophilus, allow for high rates of assimilation of nutrients from our food. Cultures such as acidophilus also act as a protective barrier against harmful cultures that may seek to invade the body. New cultures, both helpful and harmful, enter into our system through the foods we eat. When we create a healthy environment for positive cultures, they grow and proliferate. The same is true for unhealthy cultures when we create an unhealthy environment in our colon. Healthy cultures protect us from disease by standing guard in the intestines and ushering harmful cultures on their way. Often, cleansing practices such as colonics or enemas can wash away health-giving bacteria along with the fecal mucoid matter impacted on the colon. It is important to continually reintroduce healthy bacteria into the system both orally and rectally when following a colon therapy program. Fasting can also deplete the active cultures living in our system, so it is important to reintroduce cultures into the system after long water or dry fasts.

How to Culture Food

Cultured foods can be created by using a starter or by creating the ideal environment for healthy cultures to begin to grow. Because cultures are present in the air around us, there is often no need for a starter. However, using a starter is a great method to ensure you obtain the flavor you're looking for. A starter is simply a food that is already cultured. Unpasteurized kimchee or miso, for example, can be your starter for making your own batch. Following are some examples of how to make cultured foods.

STARTER METHOD (EXAMPLE: KIMCHEE)

Grind or chop 1 to 3 heads of cabbage. Add ¼ cup caraway seeds. Add 3 crushed cloves of garlic. Add the juice of 5 lemons. Add 1 tablespoon of a previous batch of kimchee or 1 teaspoon live acidophilus culture.

Place in a Harsch crock or in glass bowls for 5 to 30 days (some kimchee is aged for months), at room temperature. If using glass bowls, place the vegetables to be cultured in one bowl and put a second bowl inside it to weigh down the culturing mix (a stone or jar of water can be used as a weight), then cover with a screen or cloth to keep away any pests.

(A Harsch crock can be purchased through Loving Foods or your local Asian distributor. It is an earthen crock that has a V-ring seal on the top. This means that the mouth of the crock is fluted and water sits in the ringed V shape and the lid sits in the groove of the V, thereby sealing the crock and its contents. Air goes out but not in.)

Soak 1 cup of quinoa in a half-gallon jar for 8 hours. Drain and rinse the seeds twice daily. After 24 hours, grind the seeds with 6 cups of fresh water and place in a half-gallon jar. Let it sit for 12 hours. Drain off the rejuvelac and compost the seed pulp. Refrigerate and enjoy. (If it smells too pungent, however, don't eat it. It should smell lemony.)

Where to Obtain Cultures

Cultures can be obtained through a variety of sources. Purchase a previously made cultured food product from your local retail store or contact a health product distributor. These cultured products contain the mother or starter and can be used to create your own cultured foods at home. Some common cultured products available are:

• Kimchee from Rejuvenative Foods

• Sauerkraut from Fermentations

• Live Apple Cider Vinegar from Braggs

• Sauerkraut from Cultured

• Kombucha culture (get them from friends)

Cultures can also be purchased in their whole form (not on a substance). These are usually sold dry as a powder or as a liquid. Try to get cultures that are growing on something, because they are usually heartier and are specific to what you want to make. When buying a starter, make certain that it is refrigerated. Cultured foods are very temperature sensitive and will no longer be viable if exposed to extreme heat or cold. Here is a good source of live cultures: Gold Mine Natural Food Co. (www.goldminenaturalfoods.com).

Dehydrated Foods

Dehydrated foods, such as dried fruits, Essene bread, and dried herbs, are very concentrated. By removing the water and decreasing the mass of the food, dehydration intensifies foods and allows for the intake of a greater quantity of nutrients. Dehydrated foods are considered alive only if they are dried at or below 108°F (the point at which enzymes die and other vitamins and minerals break down). Most dried foods retain their nutrients longer than fresh because they are unaffected by the breakdown caused by water trapped within the cells. Many dried foods can also be rehydrated.

The Value of Dehydrated Foods

Dehydrated foods are concentrated nutrition. A fresh apple that might take us twenty bites to eat will take only three to seven bites to eat when it is dried. Most nuts and seeds are sold dried because it makes the oils in them more stable. Sea vegetables, fruits, and vegetables are dried for storage. Oils are considered a dried food because they come from a dried seed or nut. Spirulina is also a dried food. In fact, many South American tribes would sun dry spirulina into patties in order to carry the nutrient-rich dried food with them on their long journey across the Andes.

Dehydrated foods give us a wide range of concentrated minerals and vitamins and a concentrated amount of protein. These foods also slow down the metabolism in order to maximize assimilation. The body will rehydrate the food and take its time digesting it. Dehydrated foods can be very grounding. Often people transitioning to a raw diet find that they constantly want food. Dehydrated foods will easily fill this need by slowing the digestion and allowing for maximum absorption of both the dehydrated food and other foods that are also in the body. Dehydrated foods can be especially helpful to people who are transitioning to raw food who are used to eating a lot of starchy cooked food.

Dehydrated Foods for Travel

Dehydrated foods have always been the choice for travelers. In ancient times, people would dry part of their harvest for winter or for a long migration to warmer climates. Even today, people going to work or school will bring dried fruits or nuts because they are lightweight and stable. Dehydrated foods can be kept for considerably longer than those in fresh form. Dehydrated foods are great for hiking because of the concentrated nutrition and energy. Dried foods are often dehydrating to the body, however, so be certain to drink lots of fluids or eat fresh foods to rehydrate yourself.

Methods of Dehydrating

Dehydration is the process of removing water from food to create densely textured live foods. Each food has a different water content, so drying times vary from food to food. In ancient times, food was put in the sun to dry. Today we have more advanced technology at our disposal. Building a solar or home dehydrator is a great project and a simple way to dry food. Buying a commercial or home dehydration system unit is often the easiest and most reliable way of drying food. Enzymes die around 116°F, so to be safe, we dehydrate at around 108°F. For drying breads, I advocate the use of a dehydrator that has both a fan and a temperature control (such as Excalibur). If a dehydrator is unavailable, an oven set on the lowest temperature with the door slightly ajar will work.

The most ancient (and free) way to dehydrate food is to place it in thin layers on a ceramic or glass tray in the sun. Flipping it over frequently can help it dry faster. Another sun-drying method is to hang a hammock made of mesh or screen outside and put the food to be dried on it. If you are dehydrating outdoors in the sun, the temperature is always fine, although warmer temperatures will make dehydration occur more quickly. When making sun-baked foods, it is nice to create a screened area to do it in so that no bugs or animals get to the food. For more on drying methods and suggested times, see below.

Kissed by the Sun

The sun is the great provider of life. It is a powerful healer and giver of warmth. Most food enjoys its days basking in the sun, where it grows sweet and ripe and rich in nutrients. The sun blesses us with both light and warmth, two very powerful forms of energy. Drying foods helps concentrate even more of this powerful manna. By drying foods, we get to concentrate extra sunlight into an already sun-laden food, thereby enhancing the food with more energy.

DRYING METHODS, TIME, AND TEMPERATURE

Food	Method	Drying Time	Temperature
Apple	Sliced	13 hours	108°F
Apple	Ground	10 hours	108°F
Banana	Whole	28 hours	108°F
Banana	Sliced	18 hours	108°F
Banana	Ground	14 hours	108°F
Carrot	Ground	8 hours	108°F
Coconut	Sliced	18 hours	108°F
Coconut	Ground	21 hours	108°F
Corn	Whole	18 hours	108°F
Corn	Ground	15 hours	108°F

Food	Method	Drying Time	Temperature
Corn	Ground sprouts	15 hours	108°F
Flowers	Whole	3 to 5 hours	98°F
Garlic	Whole	12 hours	108°F
Garlic	Ground	8 hours	108°F
Herbs	Whole	5 to 7 hours	100°F
Kiwi	Sliced	16 hours	108°F
Mango	Sliced	21 hours	108°F
Melon	Ground	21 hours	108°F
Oat sprouts	Whole	15 hours	108°F
Oat sprouts	Ground	24 hours	108°F
Onion	Sliced	13 hours	108°F
Onion	Ground	10 hours	108°F
Papaya	Sliced	20 hours	108°F
Papaya	Ground	16 hours	108°F
Peach	Sliced	24 hours	108°F
Peach	Ground	18 hours	108°F
Pear	Sliced	15 hours	108°F
Pear	Ground	13 hours	108°F
Persimmon	Whole	48 hours	108°F
Persimmon	Sliced	18 hours	108°F
Persimmon	Ground	15 hours	108°F
Potato	Sliced	21 hours	108°F
Sapodilla	Sliced	12 hours	108°F
Sea veggies	Whole	15 hours	100°F
Sprouts	Whole	13 hours	100°F
Sprouts	Ground	20 hours	100°F
Star fruit	Sliced	13 hours	108°F
Sunchoke	Sliced	16 hours	108°F
Tomato	Sliced	18 hours	108°F

Raw Foods

Finding pure food has become a challenge in the modern world. Foods that are labeled "organic" can still be mass-produced, possibly using "natural" pesticides that are still toxic. (Purely natural pesticides such as bay leaves or marigolds are not harmful, but in my book, biodynamic farming—using living plants to deter bugs—is still the only way to go.) Even worse, companies may claim their food is organic when it's not just to get more money. On the flip side, there are also pure, truly natural foods that are sold without the labels and high price tags that are usually associated with organic foods; it's just that the farmers who grow and sell them can't afford certification as organic farmers.

To be absolutely sure your produce is pure, grow it yourself or forage it in the wild. Planting trees, growing a garden, and especially growing sprouts are all excellent ways to obtain food. Foraged foods are ideal since nature grew them on its own. Participating in local herb walks and interviewing docents can provide a solid education about the habitats and seasonal availability of local foods.

Farmers' markets are usually the next best source of fresh produce. They're also a great place to learn about local produce that's available for foraging. In fact, many farmers' markets have a side selection of foods that grow wild in the area; look here for information and inspiration. Farmers also sell directly from their farms, so check online for local resources and stop at local farm stands. What the farmers don't sell themselves will go to the shelf of a local store or co-op; ask around and final local markets that buy produce directly from local farms.

For exotic and hard-to-find items, check Asian or Latin American markets, as they usually carry a wide range of tropical produce and special items. There are also some companies that mail order exotic foods and fresh product directly from farms, so no matter where you live, you should be able to find a nice array of produce.

Herbs

Herbs are the greens and flowers of annually blooming plants commonly used for seasoning and medicine. They are used both fresh and dried.

BASIL: A sweet, broad-leafed aromatic herb that grows rapidly. Some varieties are purple, French, Thai, and lemon basil. Basil is commonly used in Italian and Thai cooking.

CILANTRO: A flat-leafed herb widely used in Latin American and Southeast Asian cooking. Sometimes called Mexican parsley, fresh coriander, or Chinese parsley. This plant's seeds are known as coriander.

DILL: A soft, wispy, refreshing herb.

FENNEL: A wispy herb similar in appearance to dill, with a slightly sweet licorice taste and smell.

LAMB'S QUARTER: An herb commonly found throughout the northeast and northwest areas of the United States.

LEMONGRASS: A long, hearty, sharp-edged green grass with a lemonlike scent.

LOVAGE: A sweet, beautiful flowering herb with a strong scent.

MALVA: A slightly bitter, richly green herb.

MARJORAM: A pungent and aromatic herb.

MINT: A refreshing and cool herb that's available in many varieties and grows almost anywhere.

> **Apple mint:** A sweet mint with a slightly apple taste and round leaves.
>
> **Chocolate mint:** A superbly rich mint with tiny, dark leaves.
>
> **Lemon mint:** A mild mint with a distinct lemon aroma.
>
> **Peppermint:** A strong, darkly colored mint with smooth, long leaves.
>
> **Pineapple mint:** A mild, sweet-tasting mint with a hint of pineapple.
>
> **Spearmint:** A light-colored, mild, cooling mint with pointed leaves.

OREGANO: A somewhat sharp-flavored herb available in broad-leafed or creeping forms and often used in Italian recipes.

PARSLEY: A clean-tasting, refreshing herb, high in vitamin C, that's available in curly and flat-leaf types.

PEPPERGRASS: A thin grass with a mildly spicy pepper flavor.

PURSLANE: A round-leafed herb that is quite nice in salads.

ROSEMARY: A piney, minty herb resembling evergreen needles.

SAGE: A robust, pungent, aromatic herb with long, whitish, fuzzy leaves.

SHEEP SORREL: An herb with a tangy flavor and high in vitamin C and potassium.

SOURGRASS: A wild type of sorrel with yellow flowers, a lemony flavor, and a slight bite.

TARRAGON: A tart, mild herb that tastes of anise.

THYME: An earthy-flavored herb that comes in more than forty varieties.

WINTERCRESS: An herb with a slightly spicy, slightly bitter taste, often found growing in moist areas.

Edible Flowers

There are many types of edible flowers found all over the world. They go wonderfully in salads or as garnish on any dish. Make sure you use only unsprayed, organically raised blossoms in your food. Edible flowers have a very short shelf life, so it is best to grow them yourself either in a garden outdoors or in a window box.

ARUGULA: A delicate, pale lavender or white blossom with a slightly spicy taste.

BORAGE: A blue star-shaped flower with a mild, watery, cucumber flavor.

CALENDULA: A yellow-orange flower that is sweet and calming to the nervous system. It is also known as pot marigold.

CHRYSANTHEMUM: A silvery white flower with a slightly spicy taste.

DAYLILY: A yellow-orange flower. The petals of this plant are edible, while the young buds are not. Daylilies have a nutty, sweet taste.

GARLIC: A white or purple flower from the garlic chive with a spicy, garlicky taste.

GERANIUM: A mild-tasting flower available in many varieties, such as rose, lemon, almond, and mint.

HIBISCUS: A bright red, orange, or pink flower that makes wonderful sun tea.

HONEYSUCKLE: A deliciously sweet, honey-flavored, yellow-white tiny flower.

IMPATIENS: A five-petaled pastel-colored flower with a mildly sweet taste.

LAVENDER: A flower with a blue-purple blossom that tastes almost as strong as it smells.

NASTURTIUM: A very spicy flower available in a variety of colors, from yellow to bright red.

PANSY: A velvety-textured, mild-flavored flower available in many colors.

RED CLOVER: A purple-and-white-topped flower that can be grown from clover seed or found in fields in the early summer. This herb contains high quantities of vitamin C.

ROSE: A soft, sweet, aromatic flower.

SCOTCH BROOM: A sweet, honey-flavored, bright yellow flower.

SQUASH: A tender, huge, orange flower with a sweet and slightly starchy taste.

TIGER LILY: An exquisite orange flower that tastes like sweet crispy lettuce.

VIOLET: A purple-pink flower with both sweet and spicy overtones. The flowers, stems, and leaves of the violet are all edible and contain vitamins A and C.

Sea Vegetables

Sea vegetables have an abundance of minerals and trace elements. They are an ideal source of organic salts. They are high in calcium, iodine, potassium, magnesium, phosphorus, iron, niacin, and vitamins A, B_1, B_2, B_6, B_{12}, and C. Sea vegetables are very helpful in cleaning the prostate and the whole lymphatic system. Although eating fresh sea vegetables is ideal, sea vegetables can be purchased dried and then soaked to rehydrate.

Some companies boil their vegetables before drying them. Check the labels carefully; if they don't specify that the vegetables were or were not boiled, find another brand or call the company's customer service number and ask. Always read the package and look for kosher certification to verify that it contains no animal or fish products. Purchase dried sea vegetables at Asian markets or directly from Gold Mine Natural Food Co. (www.goldminenaturalfoods.com).

AGAR-AGAR: A clear, gelatinous seaweed product available in flakes or bars. Agar-agar is used to gel liquids into a more solid form.

ARAME: A dark brownish green, broad-leafed sea plant most commonly shredded into fine strands. This sweet, nutty sea vegetable is abundant in calcium, phosphorus, iodine, iron, potassium, and vitamins A and B. (Grows around Japan, the Pacific coasts, and South America.)

DULSE: A leafy purple sea frond from cold northern Atlantic waters that can be eaten dried or rehydrated. Its flat, fan-shaped fronds have a chewy consistency. Dulse has a very high concentration of iron. It is an excellent source of magnesium and potassium and is quite rich in iodine; calcium; phosphorus; vitamins A, B₂, B₆, C, E; and many trace minerals. (Grows in cold waters worldwide.)

HIJIKI: A stringy black seaweed that looks like twine. It is thicker and stronger-tasting than arame and is very high in calcium. It also has ample amounts of vitamins A, B₁, B₂; phosphorus; and iron. (It grows in waters around southern Japan, Hawaii, Taiwan, and the Indian Ocean.)

KOMBU (kelp): A green seaweed with chewy, sweetish blades that is dried and used as a condiment or flavor enhancer. Kombu is rich in potassium, sodium, and vitamins A and B. Monosodium glutamate (MSG) is derived from kombu. Dried kelp is available in strips, flakes, and in powdered form as well as vinegared and shredded, giving it a breadlike flavor. (Found in cold waters worldwide, including Japan, northern and mid-Pacific coast, and Atlantic coast.)

NORI: A bright light purple when growing, this flat-bladed sea vegetable dries purple or black-green. Nori is most commonly found shredded and pressed into sheets and used in sushi. Nori is an excellent source of calcium, potassium, manganese, magnesium, and phosphorus and is especially rich in niacin and protein. Nori also contains large amounts of vitamins A and C. (Grows in the colder waters of the Atlantic and Pacific and along the coasts of Japan, California, Hawaii, the Philippines, and Europe.)

SEA PALM: A sea frond that is gray-green with vertical ridges. It is quite firm and slightly jellylike. (Found on the western North American rocky coastline.)

WAKAME: A dark green seaweed that is sweet and becomes a beautiful light green when rehydrated. It is quite slippery when wet. Wakame is an abundant source of calcium and niacin and is high in vitamins A, B₁, B₂, and C. (Grows in northern Japan, the United States, and the British Isles.)

Algae

An organism that transforms sunlight into chlorophyll, algae is known for its blood-building and cleaning properties. Algae is abundant in trace minerals and is very digestible and easily assimilated because of its simplicity. Many people use algae supplements for their high amino acid content, naturally available protein, and high levels of trace minerals. The powder and liquid forms of single-celled algae are the only raw options; algae flakes contain soy lecithin, which in its preparation is steamed at temperatures of 140°F and higher.

CHLORELLA: A powdered algae originally discovered by Christopher Hills and Hirashi Nakamura, renowned scientists whose research provided a lot of information about algae to the West.

PHYTOPLANKTON: A sea variety of algae that grows in deep waters and still produces chlorophyll from water-filtered sunlight. Phytoplankton is no longer commercially available.

SPIRULINA: A spiral-shaped algae known for its potency and easy digestibility. Dried spirulina powder is the highest source of protein known, containing almost 70 percent fully absorbable protein.

Mushrooms

Not all mushrooms are fit for raw consumption. Use caution when harvesting any wild mushrooms. Mushrooms can provide a rich and meaty texture that is satisfying to people transitioning to a vegetarian diet.

CHICKEN-OF-THE-WOODS: A thick, yellow-orange, many-layered tree fungus with a fibrous texture. Used fresh.

ENOKI (enokidake): A tiny, slim, white mushroom that frequently grows in clusters. Used fresh.

HEN-OF-THE-WOODS: A light gray tree fungus that grows in bunches similar to chicken-of-the-woods. Used fresh.

KOMBUCHA: A flat fungus grown in a jar or tank of water with green tea and a sweetener. A well-cared-for kombucha colony will continuously divide and multiply, producing an endless supply of kombucha-infused tea if desired. Kombucha tea is known for its healing properties.

MOREL: A spongy, wrinkly, brown-black wild mushroom with an elongated head. Used fresh and dried.

PORTOBELLO: A large, tender mushroom with a smooth white-brown surface and white stem. Used fresh.

SHIITAKE: A small butter-flavored mushroom used in Asian recipes. Used fresh and dried.

SILVER EAR: A silver-white fungus that looks like a sponge or coral. Used fresh and dried.

STRAW: A very fleshy mushroom. Used fresh (avoid canned).

TREE EAR: A dark, round fungus. The smaller varieties are known to be the tastiest. Used fresh.

TRUFFLES: A very rare (and therefore expensive) wild delicacy. A must for the mushroom connoisseur. Used fresh and dried.

WOOD EAR: A small gold-brown fungus with a woody flavor. Used fresh.

Legumes

Also known as beans, legumes grow in pods, usually on vines.

ADZUKI BEAN: A red-skinned dried bean with a sweet flavor when sprouted.

BLACK BEAN: A dried black bean with a starchy flavor when sprouted.

GARBANZO BEAN (chickpea): A beige, dimpled dried bean, very good for sprouting.

KIDNEY BEAN: A variety of red-skinned legumes that are kidney shaped. These dried beans have a bland taste when sprouted.

LENTILS: A traditional ingredient in Indian cuisine, the lentil is a small, flat, and round bean that is sold dried. Lentils come in many colors, are high in protein, and make for very sweet sprouts.

    Green lentil: When sprouted, good in salads.

    Red lentil: Use sprouted in soups and sauces.

    Yellow lentil: Good for making sprout loaves and pâtés.

LIMA BEAN: A large green-yellow, kidney-shaped bean, with a sweet taste when fresh. Available both fresh and dried.

MUNG BEAN: A fresh, yellow- or green-skinned bean whose sprouts are used frequently in Asian cuisine.

NAVY BEAN: A white dried bean with a mild taste when sprouted.

PEA: A green, round legume with a deliciously sweet flavor when fresh. Dried varieties are also available. Also makes great sprouts.

PEANUT: A legume often referred to as a nut, this fresh bean has a rich nutty flavor.

POLE BEAN: A fresh, long pod bean that is crisp and sweet.

SNAP PEA: A fresh, superbly sweet bean. These crunchy little bright green pods are delicious in salads.

SNOW PEA: A traditional Chinese pea pod that is sold fresh and is slightly blander than the snap pea.

SOYBEAN: A powerhouse of protein, the soybean is extremely versatile. In either fresh or dried form, the soybean provides the basis for tofu, soymilk, miso, tamari, and many other products.

STRING BEAN: A fresh, long, thin, crispy, green pod with small beans inside.

WAX BEAN: A fresh, long, thin, yellow pod similar to the string bean.

Greens

Leafy green plants grow in heads in a huge array of colors, flavors, and textures. They are rich in chlorophyll, silica, and fiber.

ARUGULA: A peppery green with a slightly spicy flavor.

BAMBOO SHOOTS: The young shoots of certain types of bamboo are edible.

BEET GREENS: A plant with dark green leaves with a red vein. It tastes mildly bitter, with a woodsy flavor.

BELE (tree spinach): A plant from the Philippines with large, broad leaves. This plant's tough gelatinous leaves are almost 30 percent silica and are great for rolling burritos.

CHARD: A member of the beet family, chard has coarse leaves and a woodsy taste.

CHICORY: A dark green plant (often found in the wild) with narrow, frilly leaves; a pale green center; and a bitter flavor.

COMFREY: A plant with broad fuzzy leaves that can aid in cellular regeneration and the healing of wounds and muscle and bone injuries. Best for raw consumption when the leaves are young and tender.

CURLY ENDIVE: A crisp, compact head with frilly light green to white leaves and a slightly bitter flavor.

DANDELION: A bitter green with small and narrow dark leaves. Look for dandelions growing in the wild.

ESCAROLE: Less bitter, and with broader and curlier leaves than endive, escarole is part of the chicory family.

FIDDLEHEAD FERN: Often wild, this young sprouted fern has curly light fronds and a delectably nutty asparagus-like flavor.

FRISÉE: A bitter, light yellow to white salad green with curly leaves.

GREEN BUTTER LETTUCE: A crispy, large-headed lettuce with generous, wide leaves.

GREEN LEAF LETTUCE: A loose-headed green with frilly edges and a mild taste.

GREEN OAK LETTUCE: A loose-headed green with frilly, tapering finger leaves.

KATUK: An African tree whose leaves are more than 30 percent protein and taste like nuts.

MÂCHE: A mild and delicate green with small round leaves.

MALABAR SPINACH: A purple and green variety of garden spinach.

MIZUNA: A jagged-leafed, slightly spicy green often used in Asian foods.

MUSTARD: A very pungent, spicy, tart green abundant in vitamins A and B.

NEW ZEALAND SPINACH: A crispy vinelike spinach that grows wild.

PLANTAIN: A long-leaved plant that is common in North America.

RADICCHIO: A type of red chicory, radicchio has a loose white head and tangy crimson leaves.

RED BUTTER LETTUCE: A crispy, large-headed lettuce with a red tinge.

RED CHARD: A large, leafy green with a red vein running up its middle. A member of the beet family.

RED HIBISCUS: These burgundy-colored leaves have a lemony taste. Red hibiscus can often be found growing in the wild.

RED OAK LETTUCE: A loose-headed green with frilly, red-tinged, tapering, fingerlike leaves.

RED ORACH: A blossoming burgundy-colored green with mild flavor.

SAVORY: A distinctly peppery green with a spicy flavor.

SPINACH: A deep green plant whose delicate leaves have a rich, earthy flavor.

TANGO: A pungent and flavorful green with a rich flavor.

TAT SOI: A round, crispy green with a sweet taste.

TRAVISSIO: A sweet and spicy green.

WATERCRESS: A round-leafed, fast-growing green with a bitter aftertaste.

Roots

Roots are starchy, nourishing plants that grow underground. Most root greens are edible and highly nutritious. A root can be cut into a few pieces that, if put in the ground, will each grow new full roots (provided each piece includes some portion of the root's external surface).

BEETS: A large, bulbous root with red and green leaves.

Chioggia: A red-and-white-ringed beet that looks tie-dyed inside.

Golden: A golden variety that makes a beautiful decoration.

Red: A common variety of beet quite high in iron.

CARROT: A long orange root with a wispy green top.

CELERY: A large root with multiple stalks that are high in water and organic sodium content and have small leafy greens on the tips.

CHINESE ARTICHOKE: A small white root.

GINGER: A beige root, grown in riverbeds, with a sweet and spicy flavor.

GINSENG: A gummy root in a variety of colors. Especially valued for its energy-boosting and yang-tonifying characteristics.

JICAMA: A large light-brown root with a white, crispy inside.

LOTUS: A conical tuber that contains hollow tubes in a ring.

PARSNIP: A bitter, white root—very nice when shredded.

POTATOES: A smooth-skinned, eye-covered root that grows prolifically.

Golden russet: A golden watery potato (very starchy raw).

Purple: A dark-skinned, purple-fleshed dry potato.

Red romano: A red-skinned, white-fleshed, very starchy potato.

RADISHES

Daikon: A long, large, white, crispy, spicy root.

Horseradish: A very spicy white root.

Red: A round, red-skinned, juicy radish.

White: A slightly spicier version of the red.

RUTABAGA: A purple-and-white-skinned crispy root with a watery taste.

SALSIFY: A brown, long, skinny, slightly hairy root.

SWEET POTATO: An orange-fleshed, very sweet root.

TARO: A dense tuber that causes intense mouth and throat discomfort when eaten raw.

TURMERIC: A pungent, bitter, orange root used often in Indian food.

TURNIP: A spicy and bitter, large, round, white root.

YAM: A root very similar to the sweet potato in taste and appearance.

YUCCA: A plant also known as cassava that is too dense and starchy to eat raw.

Brassica

These hardy plants grow in cooler climates in clusters flanked by leaves. They are coated with layers of acidophilus, which helps increase intestinal flora.

BROCCOLI: A green, clustered, flowerlike plant with some purple overtones that is very high in calcium.

BRUSSELS SPROUT: A plant that looks like miniature, tight cabbages growing on a stalk.

CABBAGES: An acidophilus-rich plant that grows in cooler climates.

   Bok choy (*Chinese chard*): A cabbage with thick white stalks and broad, dark green leaves.

   Choy sum: A cabbage similar to bok choy with a more slender appearance.

   Miniature red: A smaller version of the normal red.

   Napa (*Chinese cabbage*): A plant with layers of dark green, purple-veined leaves.

   Red: A cabbage with deep magenta leaves on a compact head.

   Savoy: A cabbage with crinkly, pale green leaves and a loose head.

   White: A dense, firm head with smooth yellow-green leaves.

CAULIFLOWER: A white, flowerlike plant with a creamy taste.

KALE: A dark green to purple plant with overlapping leaves and red-purple veins.

KOHLRABI: A round and green plant with a purple stem.

TURNIP: A plant with tart leaves and a spicy root.

Allium

Allium are pungent bulblike plants that grow underground and produce green shoots. They are anthelmintic, which means they help remove intestinal parasites.

ASPARAGUS: A plant with long branches that end in flowerlike tops with a robust taste.

CHIVE: A delicate, slender, mild-tasting plant with an onion flavor.

GARLIC: A white-skinned bulb composed of cloves individually wrapped in a parchmentlike membrane and with a spicy, often strong flavor.

LEEK: A grasslike plant with a slight onion flavor.

ONIONS

Kula: An oblong, very sweet onion with a white interior and yellow skin.

Red: A spicy onion with purple-red skin.

Spanish: A yellow-skinned, slightly spicy round onion.

White: A crisp and sweet onion with a white skin.

SCALLION: A long, green, grasslike shoot.

SHALLOT: A small brown bulb with a taste between that of garlic and onion.

Nightshades

Nightshade plants, which grow at night, produce a fruit with fine-lobed ears and edible flowers of various colors.

ARTICHOKE: A flowerlike green plant with sharp leaves.

EGGPLANT: A large purple fruit with a light green interior with seeds.

OKRA: A pointed, cylindrical fruit that can be green to purple.

PEPPERS

Hot

Anaheim: A long, mild, thin, fresh green chile.

Cayenne: A long and twisting orange to red, pointed, dried chile.

Chile: A small, round-tipped red pepper.

Chipotle: A smoked and dried jalapeño with a smoky flavor and spicy aftertaste.

Habanero: An extremely hot fresh chile whose small size belies its fiery taste.

Jalapeño: A medium-sized fresh green chile with a nice, gentle spice.

Scotch bonnet: An orange, bell-shaped, very hot fresh chile.

Tepin: A medium-hot red to green dried chile.

Thai: A tiny red-purple pepper that's super-spicy.

Sweet

Green: A crispy, watery bell pepper.

Orange: A pepper that, aside from its color, is very similar to the red.

Purple: A bland, almost bitter, purple-skinned bell pepper.

Red: A very sweet and crunchy bell pepper.

Yellow: A very sweet and quite juicy bell pepper.

TOMATOES

Beefsteak: A large, watery, light red to pink tomato.

Cherry: A tiny, round, very sweet and juicy tomato.

Pear: A small pear-shaped tomato that grows in a variety of colors.

Plum: A medium-sized red tomato, great for slicing.

Cucurbits (Vine Squash and Melons)

Cucurbits are fruits that grow on vines and contain many seeds. All flowers from cucurbits are edible.

ACORN SQUASH: A large green and brown squash resembling an acorn.

MELONS

Cantaloupe: This common melon has fairly dense orange to pink flesh with beige skin that is scaly or bumpy.

Crenshaw: A scaly-skinned, golden-fleshed melon that is the ultimate in juiciness.

French: A golden orange-fleshed melon with smooth beige skin that is very sweet.

Honeydew: A smooth, firm, green-yellow-skinned melon with pale green flesh that is ultrasweet.

Muskmelon: A melon with scaly, netted skin and extremely sweet yellow-orange to yellow-green flesh.

Sharlyn: A melon with skin like a cantaloupe, this ultrasweet melon has golden-orange flesh.

Sugar baby: A delectable, smaller, ultrasweet, seedless version of watermelon.

Watermelon: A large melon with smooth skin that is green or dark yellow, either mottled or striped. The crisp flesh, from pink to red, is composed of 96 percent water. A great kidney cleaner.

Yellow baby: A strain of watermelon that has a creamy yellow flesh.

PUMPKIN: A large, rounded, orange squash with many seeds.

YELLOW SQUASH: A sweet and crunchy yellow-skinned summer squash with a mild taste.

ZUCCHINI: A long green summer squash with an earthy flavor.

Seeds

A seed is defined by the fact that its hull can be removed, and that it produces two leaves upon sprouting. Seeds are the potential energy source of plants-to-be and as such have highly increased nutritional value. Seeds can be used in a variety of forms. Store-bought seeds are a dried food and are concentrated. If seeds are soaked, their enzyme inhibitors release and they become more digestible. This can also be accomplished by grinding a seed into powder or by chewing very well. Sprouting seeds is a great way to get more bang for your buck: it increases the seeds' nutritional value as well as their size, thereby providing more food mass.

ALFALFA: A seed that sprouts quickly and provides many valuable nutrients.

BUCKWHEAT: A black-hulled grain that produces sweet greens. Buckwheat is the highest in protein of any seed.

CELERY: A seed that helps inhibit molds and is useful to add to other seeds for sprouting.

CHIA: A seed that produces a gelatinous coating before sprouting and is packed with energy.

CLOVER: A seed that provides a chlorophyll-rich sprout.

CORIANDER: A seed with a mildly spicy flavor.

CUMIN: A robust-tasting seed that is quite earthy.

FENNEL: A seed with a distinctive licorice flavor.

FENUGREEK: This seed produces a rich and tasty sprout that is great in salads.

FLAX: A seed that creates a gelatinous coating when soaked. Provides a good balance of omega oils and essential fatty acids and works well as an egg substitute.

GARLIC: A very spicy seed with a reddish hue when sprouted.

HEMP: A rich, tangy seed, high in essential fatty acids.

MUSTARD: A versatile seed that makes great sprouts and is used dry as a spice.

ONION: A sweet and spicy seed, great for sprouting.

POPPY: A round blue seed with a delightfully crunchy texture.

PUMPKIN: A very robust and sweet seed that provides a good balance of omega oils and essential fatty acids.

RADISH: A spicy and bitter seed, good for sprouting.

SESAME: A very sweet, tiny white seed.

SUNFLOWER: A pointed gray seed, great for making Essene bread and pâtés.

WILD RICE: Black long-grain wild rice is the only rice that is a seed and not a grain. This seed also sprouts without any oxygen.

Grains

Grains are the kernel of a plant that produces only one shoot, a grass. Grains are permanently affixed to their hull and usually contain gluten. These close relatives of seeds are abundant in carbohydrates and most digestible when sprouted.

AMARANTH: Native to the Americas and the second-smallest grain, amaranth plants grow soft red and white flowers. The seeds sprout easily.

CORN: A starchy, sweet, juicy grain that grows in a number of colors. Wonderful both raw and sprouted.

MILLET: A small yellow grain with starchy taste when sprouted.

OAT: A very sweet grain to sprout. Lots of fiber.

QUINOA: A grain worshipped by the Aztecs, quinoa is the third smallest grain and creates a spicy sprout.

RICE: The staple grain of China. Most rices are edible when sprouted, though not very tasty. Experiment with the length of sprout time for varied flavors.

Basmati: A translucent long grain.

Brown long grain: A long, round, brown grain.

Brown short grain: A short, stubby brown grain.

Jasmine: A sweet white rice with a delicate fragrance.

Spanish: A long yellow rice.

Sushi: A round white grain used in the making of sushi.

Sweet: A white, stubby grain.

RYE: A brown seed good for making Essene bread.

TEFF: A very small grain, sweet and gray. High in protein.

WHEAT: A grass rich in chlorophyll. The staple grain of America, it produces a tasty sprout.

Hard winter: A good variety for growing wheatgrass.

Soft winter: A wheat that is very good for making Essene bread.

Summer: A sweeter wheat variety. Good for making breads and salads.

Nuts

Nuts are the inner center of a fruit that is contained by a shell. Nuts are very sweet when harvested and get much more oily when dried.

ALMOND: A white oblong nut, pointed on one end, that comes in a beige shell.

BRAZIL: A creamy, oily nut that is often an inch in length.

CASHEW: A white, very sweet, crescent-shaped nut that is poisonous unless dried in the sun.

CHESTNUT: A brown-skinned, large, round, crunchy nut that is sometimes bitter.

HAZELNUT: A dark brown–skinned, small, round nut with a rich flavor.

MACADAMIA: A sweet white nut with a delightful crunch and a very hard shell.

MALABAR CHESTNUT: A light brown–skinned, sweet nut that is crispy when sprouted.

PECAN: An oblong-shelled nut with a wavy interior. This nut is very sweet.

PINE: A tiny golden teardrop-shaped seed from a pinecone. It tastes quite rich.

WALNUT: A round-shelled and warp-shaped nut.

Fruits

Fruit is a beautiful, colorful, delicious membrane made of cells filled with organic water and nutrients. Fruit is love since it is designed to feed the seed inside it or to feed a creature and, with that creature's cooperation, spread the seeds, making more fruit trees and more fruit. Fruits come in a huge variety of flavors and colors.

ANNONA OR MOYA FAMILY: Annonaceous fruits have scaly skins, black seeds, and creamy flesh.

Atemoya: A hybrid between the sweetsop and cherimoya.

Bullock's heart: A purple-skinned fruit consisting of an exterior with rounded scales and an interior flesh that is sweet and creamy.

Cherimoya: A sweet and juicy version of the sweetsop, with far fewer seeds.

Rollinia deliciosa: A spiky black and gold fruit with the sweet flavor of lemon pudding.

Soursop: A spiky green fruit also known as the guanabana, with a sweet-and-sour white flesh and many poisonous seeds that must be removed before consumption.

Sweetsop: A green, round, scaly fruit also known as the sugar apple, with a seed-filled interior and a sweet and creamy taste.

APPLES

Discovery: A red apple that fruits late in the season.

Gala: A medium-sized, crisp, juicy apple, with a skin that is mostly red with some yellow.

Golden Delicious: A golden, sun-filled apple with a sweet taste.

Granny Smith: A hard green apple with a sweet-tart taste.

Jonagold: A golden apple with a mild flavor.

McIntosh: A small red and white apple that is good when soft.

Pippin: A crispy and crunchy apple with red skin.

Red Delicious: A large red apple with a sweet flavor and a hard crunch.

Spartan: A medium-sized red and green apple with a mildly sour taste.

Starking Delicious: A small red and gold apple.

ASIAN PEAR: A sweet beige-skinned fruit that has a taste and texture similar to a pear but looks like an apple.

AVOCADOS

Alligator pear: A watery, light-colored, small, slender avocado.

Bacon: A rich bacon-flavored avocado with smooth dark green skin.

Cocktail avocado: A sweet avocado that is the smallest of its kind.

Common: A round, hard-skinned avocado with a creamy interior.

Ettinger: A green, somewhat rough-skinned avocado with a creamy interior.

Fuerte: A watery avocado with smooth skin that's sometimes purple.

Haas: A dark, rough-skinned avocado with a buttery taste. One of the most popular varieties.

Nabal: A large purple avocado whose flavor varies from tree to tree.

Reed: A round, green-skinned, sweet and creamy avocado.

Sharwil: A green-skinned, dry, buttery avocado.

BANANAS

Apple: A small starchy banana with a reddish interior.

Bluefield: This is the largest, fattest, and sweetest of its kind.

Chinese: A large and very sweet banana. Slightly thinner than the Bluefield variety.

Cuban red: A red semistarchy, semisweet banana.

Dessert: A medium-sized sweet and creamy banana.

Ice cream: A large triangular banana with white flesh reminiscent of vanilla ice cream.

Lady finger: A tiny and supersweet banana.

Plantain: A dry and starchy banana.

BERRIES

Black raspberry: A medium-sized berry formed of many black beads.

Blackberry: A black seed–filled berry with a very strong, slightly sour taste.

Blueberry: A small blue bush berry with a sweet taste. A very high source of pectin.

Boysenberry: A sweet purple berry.

Cranberry: A very tangy and sour red berry.

Currant

Black: A very sweet berry often eaten dried.

Red: A slightly more tart red variety

White: A whitish-yellow variety.

Dewberry: A sweet, tiny cousin of the raspberry.

Gooseberry: A green bush berry related to the blueberry.

Mulberry: A black berry that has a sweet-and-sour flavor and grows on trees.

Physalis fruits

Chinese lantern: A tiny, yellow, sweet, tomatolike fruit coated with a papery skin.

Tomatillo: A green, tart, tomatolike fruit, also covered with a papery husk.

Raspberry: A red, very sweet, oblong fruit from a bush that grows in cold climates.

Strawberry: A pointed red berry that has a distinct taste and grows on low shrubs.

Alpine: A white variety that's not as sweet as the traditional strawberry.

Hot boy: A very crimson berry with a tart bite.

Red gauntlet: A large red variety with a high sugar content.

Scarlet: A dark red, very sweet, medium-sized berry.

White: A tiny white to yellow berry.

Wild: A miniature berry with little flavor that grows in small clusters in the shade.

Tayberry: A very sweet and mild berry also known as the thimbleberry.

BREADFRUIT: A round, scaly fruit that tastes like bread pudding when eaten very ripe.

CACAO: Food of the gods. Cacao pods, ranging in color from yellow to purple and resembling a papaya in shape, contain both a sweet white pulp and a number of small seeds. The seeds, when dried and roasted, are the source of chocolate.

CAROB: Carob pods are nature's candy bars: they taste like chocolate-covered caramel. The seeds are as hard as rocks, so remove them before eating or navigate around them carefully.

CHERRIES

Barbados: A small black cherry with a large seed.

Bing: A very tangy cherry.

Dukes: A large black cherry with a rich taste.

Early Rivers: A red cherry that is quite sweet.

Surinam: A small, light red, sour cherry shaped like a small pumpkin.

Calamondin: A tiny, very sour orange.

Citron: A medium-sized yellow fruit with lemony flavor.

Kumquat: A small orange fruit with a sweet and sour flavor.

Lemon: A sour fruit with golden juice and skin.

Ugli fruit: A rough-skinned version of the lemon.

Meyer lemon: A sweeter and juicier lemon.

Limes

Green: A green-skinned fruit with sour flavor and sweet undertones.

Kaffir: A small pear-shaped lime, whose leaves, which are uniquely shaped like two leaves joined end to end, are often used in Asian cuisine.

Tiny: A small, round, yellow to green lime.

Yellow: A yellow-orange variety.

Orangequat: A sour orange with mild flavor.

CITRUS, SWEET

Grapefruits

Pink grapefruit: A slightly more sour version of the red.

Pomelo: A very large and thick-skinned grapefruit.

Ruby red: A red-fleshed, very sweet variety of grapefruit.

Oranges

Blood: A red-and-orange-skinned, very sweet fruit.

Clementine: A tangy and juicy orange.

Mandarin: A tangy and tart orange.

Mineola: A very juicy sweet orange.

Navel: A very round and mild orange.

Satsuma: A small Asian variety with a tangy aftertaste.

Seville: A sweet golden-fleshed variety.

Sour: A sour version of the navel orange.

Tangelo: A cross between a tangerine and an orange.

Tangerine: A very dark orange in color, with soft, sweet fruit. Resembles a squished orange.

Unique fruit: A rough-skinned sour fruit.

Valencia: A very common variety that is easy to cultivate.

COCONUT: A hard-shelled fruit of a palm tree that contains both water that is high in electrolytes and a white gelatinous meat that is very rich and packed with protein.

Coconuts are the fruit of a palm tree that has been around since prehistoric times. This prolific plant has made it to the shore of every continent except Antarctica and is available in more than 100 varieties. Coconuts can float for three months in the ocean, land on a sandy beach, and still sprout up a tree that will bear up to ten thousand coconuts in its lifetime.

Coconuts can be used at almost any stage of ripeness. Baby or bitter coconuts are used for their water, as they have not yet developed any meat. The water in these young nuts is slightly bitter and is considered medicinal in many island nations around the world as well as throughout Asia. As they develop slightly sweeter water and a small amount of clear jelly on the inside of their shell, baby coconuts are then called jelly nuts or spooners. Next, they become young or green coconuts, the most popular variety for use in food and for drinking. These young nuts have very sweet water and a coating of rich, creamy, soft meat a centimeter or more thick on their inside shell.

Mature coconuts are the kind most people are used to seeing in supermarkets. These brown nuts have had most of the husk removed down to the shell layer. These nuts are old and the water either is bad or has fermented and tastes like coconut champagne. Mature coconuts are used for oil and cream made from the hard meat. If a mature nut falls to the ground and has a chance to germinate, it becomes a coconut sprout—once considered the most powerful food in the Hawaiian Islands. Sprouted coconuts contain a spongelike heart that tastes like cotton candy. Its meat, known as copra, is very thin and crispy and has a thin layer of natural coconut oil. The oil can be obtained (for nutritional, medicinal, or cosmetic purposes) just by rubbing a finger on the inside of the copra. Coconuts are essential to the raw food diet, so it is important to know how to find them at the desired ripeness and then, of course, how to open them. Since there are so many varieties of coconuts, it can be challenging to tell what stage of ripeness a coconut is at. Look for the three nubs at the base of the nut; if they're close together, the coconut is most likely young (as the nut ages, the nubs spread farther apart). High moisture content in the coconut's husk can also help determine how young a nut is; the higher the moisture content, the younger the coconut, since the husk dries out as it ages. Though most young nuts have a green stage, don't be thrown off by color: some nuts are always red, brown, gold, or green.

To open a coconut, using a machete or heavy knife, shave one side of the coconut's outer layer at a 45-degree angle until a hole providing access to the coconut water is created. Reserve or drink the water, then chop the coconut in half lengthwise with the grain. Some industrious people also open coconuts with power drills. At Chinese and Mexican markets, you may find young coconuts sold with their husks removed; typically, these nuts don't keep as long or taste as fresh, but they are much easier to open. The meat of mature nuts can be scooped out by using the back edge of a butter knife, carefully avoiding the hard shell, which isn't fun to eat. To remove the meat from a young coconut, all that's needed is a spoon since the meat is thinner and softer.

COFFEE: A small red bean of a tropical tree.

DATES: The fruit of a palm tree that, when fruiting, produces up to three hundred pounds at a time. Dates are used as the primary sweetener in a raw food diet. Dates range in color from green to golden brown to black, depending on their ripeness and variety. My favorite varieties are Bahari, for their wonderful flavor, and Medjool, for their large size and nice texture. No matter the variety, choose soft dates, as they're more likely to be fresh and have a better flavor.

Bahari: A very sweet, soft, almost honeylike date.

Bread: A very dry, chewy date.

Deglet Noor: A large and creamy variety.

Halawi: A brown, soft, sweet date.

Honey: A sticky, golden, honey-flavored date.

Medjool: A very sweet date that is one of the largest.

Zahidi: A small, dark date that has a hint of maple flavor.

DURIAN: A yellow fruit that smells like sulfur but tastes like vanilla ice cream.

FIG: A very sweet, small, plump, pear-shaped fruit filled with many seeds and small fibers. This fruit is delicious fresh and also can be dried. Dried figs are even sweeter, and often the fig sugars will crystallize on the outside.

GUAVAS

Common guava: A hard yellow-skinned fruit with pinkish flesh and many seeds.

Pineapple guava: Also known as the feijoa, a guava that tastes like pineapple.

Quince: A pear-shaped fruit also known as the guava pear.

Strawberry guava: A tiny red guava filled with a tart white membrane.

JABOTICABA: A small black-skinned fruit that is very sweet and grows directly from the trunk of a tree.

JACKFRUIT: A large, spiky fruit weighing up to seventy pounds that has an edible membrane surrounding a seed that tastes like Juicy Fruit gum.

KIWI: A small, brown, hairy fruit with distinctive bright green and black inside and a taste that is a cross between strawberry and banana. Peel before eating.

LONGAN: A fruit also known as the dragon's eye, with hard brown skin and a white membrane-covered seed that is quite juicy.

LYCHEE: A red, rough-skinned fruit similar to the longan although sweeter.

MABOLO: A fruit known as the velvet apple, with a velvety skin and a flavor like apples and bananas.

MANGOS: A sweet and juicy fruit that is grown in hundreds of varieties around the world and ranges greatly in shape, color, and flavor.

Alphonso: A juicy, orange mango with a honeylike taste.

Haden: A sticky, sweet, very orange mango with multicolored flesh.

Julie: A small, sweet mango with mild flavor.

Kent: A cold-climate mango with creamy flavor.

MANGOSTEEN: Known as the "queen of the fruits," it has a purple skin and a number of white, gelatinous, moon-shaped seeds inside.

MIRACLE FRUIT: A tiny red fruit that, when eaten before sour foods, makes them taste sweet for about thirty minutes.

MONSTERA: The large, tubular fruit of the *Monstera deliciosa* plant, with many green scales. It can only be eaten a little at a time to avoid stinging from the acids in the fruit. It tastes like pineapple and banana.

PAPAYAS: A pear-shaped fruit that contains many black seeds and takes nine months to ripen.

Babaco: A giant, mountain papaya that is mild in flavor.

Common: A yellow-skinned and yellow-fleshed, very sweet papaya.

Strawberry: A red-fleshed version that is much sweeter than other varieties.

PASSION FRUITS

Common: a yellow-shelled fruit filled with sweet-sour, yellow membrane surrounding many edible seeds.

Purple: A purple-shelled variety with a slightly more acidic taste.

Velvet: A very sweet, orange, soft-skinned passion fruit with white membranes.

PEANUT BUTTER FRUIT: A small red fruit, also known as ciruela, that tastes similar to peanut butter.

PEARS

> **Anjou:** A large green pear.
>
> **Bartlett:** A red-skinned, very sweet pear.
>
> **Bosc:** A beige-skinned pear best eaten when soft.

PERSIMMONS: A sweet orange fruit commonly grown in Asia and California.

> **Fuyu:** A round variety that is like an apple when eaten hard and like a Hachiya (below) when soft.
>
> **Hachiya:** A pointed variety that is only eaten when soft. Hachiya are very gelatinous and sweet.

PINEAPPLES: The very juicy and sweet fruit of a small ground bush with sharp leaves. It is known as the "king of the fruits" because of its crown.

> **Common:** A variety that grows rapidly and produces medium-sized fruits.
>
> **Sugarloaf:** A sweet variety with a beautiful golden color.
>
> **White:** A white-fleshed pineapple that has a lower acid content than most pineapples and tastes very creamy.

PRICKLY PEAR: A fruit from a variety of cactus, it has a very sweet and melonlike flavor and is filled with seeds. This fruit comes in purple and green and contains very simple sugars that can provide quick energy. If foraging this fruit, beware of its many minuscule barbed thorns. Clean very well before use.

RAMBUTAN: A cousin of the lychee that is oblong and has red tendrils all over its exterior.

SAPOTES: A round subtropical fruit with sweet flesh and several seeds that should be removed before using. The eggfruit and sapodilla are both members of the sapote family, but the vanilla sapote (below) is not.

> **Chocolate pudding fruit:** A fruit with a creamy brown interior and green skin that tastes like a very ripe banana. It is also known as the chocolate persimmon or black sapote.
>
> **Eggfruit:** Also called a canistel or yellow sapote, a rich orange fruit that has a very cakelike meat.
>
> **Mamey:** A caramel-flavored fruit with brown skin.
>
> **Orange:** An orange-fleshed, creamy, oblong fruit.

Sapodilla: A small brown-skinned fruit, also called a chico, that tastes like cinnamon and sugar.

Vanilla: A green-skinned fruit with a white vanilla pudding–like interior.

TAMARILLO: An oblong red fruit that is also known as the tree tomato and tastes of basil and tomatoes.

TAMARIND: A rich seed with a sweet-tart flavor.

VINE FRUITS

Black grapes

Flame: a dark purple, sweet grape.

White grapes

California seedless: A seedless variety of white grape.

Italia: A strain from Italy often used for wines.

Muscat: A light green grape with a very sweet taste and small seed.

Sultana: A variety of grape often used in desserts.

Thompson seedless: A darker seedless variety.

Raw Condiments

These foods are designed to season and flavor dishes. Variety is the spice of life, so use these to enliven and enhance other foods. These are available at local health food stores.

BEET POWDER: Red beets that have been dehydrated and powdered. Excellent for coloring food.

BRAGG LIQUID AMINOS: An aged soy product used to replace salt.

CAROB POWDER: The soft inner lining of the carob pod.

CAYENNE PEPPER: Dried hot pepper available in a range of Scoville units. Those with lower Scoville units are for food; those with higher ones are for medicinal usage.

CURRY POWDER: A mixture of Indian spices, which often include cumin, coriander, and turmeric.

DRIED SHREDDED COCONUT: Dehydrated coconut meat finely shredded.

ENZYME SPRINKLE: Dehydrated green papayas and lime juice.

KELP POWDER: A dried and powdered form of kombu used as a salty seasoning.

MIRIN: A sweet Asian rice wine.

MISO: An aged and cultured soy paste.

NAMA SHOYU: A fermented soy and wheat sauce.

NIGARI: A dried form of seawater that coagulates tofu.

NUTRITIONAL YEAST: A type of yeast grown in beet sugar that contains a wide range of B vitamins, especially B_{12}, which can be challenging for vegetarians to find naturally.

OILS: Any dry nut or seed, olive, or oily fruit (such as coconuts) can be pressed for oil. Be certain to look for cold-pressed oils rather than oils that have been extracted using solvents. Also, be aware that "cold-pressed" is commonly used to describe oils that result from heating ground ingredients to 160°F before pressing. Oils don't last very long separated from their whole food; store them in a dark container (light may cause spoilage) in the refrigerator. Stable oils (like olive oil) maintain their integrity when heated; unstable oils (like flax oil) become toxic when heated. The oils listed here can be found in the refrigerated and vitamin sections of health food stores.

Avocado oil: It is quite rare to find cold-extracted avocado oil. However, avocados are often very oily on their own and can be used as a whole food replacement for other oils.

Coconut oil: Coconut oil is one of the best fats you can consume. It is delicious and creamy and can be used both in recipes and as a moisturizer.

Flax oil: Flax oil is high in essential fatty acids and is one of the healthiest oils to use. Flax has a rich taste and is a delight in sweet and savory dishes.

Hemp seed oil: Hemp seed oil has a very nutty flavor and can be used in place of flax oil. This oil is unstable and should never be heated or used in recipes that are dehydrated.

Nut and seed oils: Dried seeds and nuts can be pressed for their oils. Many commercial nut and seed oils are heated during processing and are therefore not raw. Look for cold-pressed nut and seed oils in specialty stores.

Olive oil: Olive oil is the most stable oil; it can handle slight amounts of heat and is very tasty in recipes.

Other oils: There are a wide variety of oils sold in health food stores that may be far less than healthful. Fractionated or overheated oils become rancid quickly, and some oils are even toxic for human consumption.

STEVIA: A green herb that is one hundred times sweeter than sugar and is useful as a nonfruit sweetener.

SUN-DRIED SEA SALT: This salt, the result of slowly drying seawater, looks gray and feels wet. Sun-dried sea salt contains far more minerals than table salt.

VINEGARS: Always buy vinegar that says "with the mother" on the label because that is a sure sign that it is live and raw.

> **Apple cider vinegar:** A fermented apple product with a tangy taste.

> **Red wine vinegar:** A fermented grape vinegar.

WASABI: A spicy condiment made from horseradish roots and gardenia flowers. This bright green paste is served with Japanese food. Wasabi is also available in powdered form.

Raw Warnings

These warnings are designed to educate. We make the best choices we can in each situation, and we grow as we go. Be patient, take your time, and vibrant health will follow.

Agave nectar. The nectar from the agave cactus is used by many people in the living food world as a sweetener. When harvested fresh, this sweet liquid is similar to maple water or coconut water. In order to stabilize it and concentrate the sugars, agave is heated to temperatures above 150°F. This prevents it from fermenting and turning into alcohol. Commercially available agave nectar is a cooked and processed product. It can, however, be obtained in its pure, raw form.

Anything organically grown. The label "organic" doesn't mean the food was consciously grown. Many organic farms are using conventional methods that are harmful to the environment and are farming for money rather than to produce healthy natural food. Biodynamically grown foods are more conscious, yet only foods you get from farmers or grow yourself are truly consciously grown and sustainable. On the other hand, produce that is grown locally may be organic even though it isn't labeled as such (probably because the grower didn't want to apply for and pay for the certification). And all wild food is organic unless it was grown near heavily sprayed areas. Use your best judgment when looking at produce. If it is vibrant and you feel it might be organic, there is a good chance it is. Do what is right for your body. It is better to eat what your body needs than to deprive yourself because of a label.

It is also important to store up local supplies in summer and fall for winter (unless you live in an area where it's possible to eat locally year-round), because any food that must be transported by planes, trains, boats, trucks, and cars is not truly sustainable. It has been said that 70 percent of the world's transportation is used for moving food. That's a lot of fuel and wasted time. Think globally. Eat locally.

Apples and cucumbers. To increase their shelf life and improve their visual appeal, apples and cucumbers are often waxed with a synthetic or carnauba wax. Even if these items are labeled "organic" and have been grown organically, they might be treated later by the shipping or distribution company.

Bragg Liquid Aminos. This product made only out of soybeans is still one of the most controversial "living food" products. At this point, no one knows how it is made. We do know that Paul Bragg was a health pioneer and that the other Bragg products are raw and living. There have been many questions about this product, and the answer is we still don't know. Braggs is non-GMO and supposedly "organic."

Cacao. Cacao beans, or nibs, are becoming ever more popular in the raw food scene. While cacao may have some helpful properties, such as amino acid compositions and high levels of antioxidants, it can also be toxic and cause mild hallucinations in dosages of more than forty beans. Cacao is shunned by all animals in nature, and domesticated animals that are fed cacao often contract cancer and can die of toxicity. Cacao contains a chemical very similar to caffeine that is highly addictive, acts as a stimulant on the central nervous system, and causes extreme mood swings and aggressive tendencies.

Honey. Many beekeepers harm the bees when they collect the honey. Some smoke out the bees or even fumigate the hive. Many commercial hives have all the honey removed and leave none for the bees during the winter. Tropical honey is usually the safest bet since there are always flowers around and therefore always more nectar available to collect. Some honey contains larvae (baby bees), and this is not vegan. Many beekeepers use separators to keep the queen out of the top layer so the eggs don't get laid in that honey. Be sure to get honey from a source you trust, and make sure they are using non-impregnated cells to claim their golden nectar.

Nama shoyu. This is a fermented product made from soybeans, wheat, salt, and a starter. This product is cooked before being allowed to culture. This is a living food product as long as it is unpasteurized. The *Aspergillus oryzae* culture has proliferated so much by the time you purchase it that there is more culture and very few remnants of the soy-wheat soup that the culture lived in.

Nori. Most nori contains fish! In fact, nori can contain up to 10 percent fish and still be labeled only as nori. When nori is harvested, it is caught as a big mass of sea lettuce in nets. This wet seaweed is then lightly rinsed, put in a big blender, and then spread out like paper to dry. A few companies sell Buddhist and kosher varieties of nori, which are fish-free.

Nutritional yeast. This bacteria is superabundant in B vitamins, especially B_{12}, which is often lacking in a vegetarian diet. Some companies freeze-dry their yeast, although most kiln-dry it at 375°F for three seconds. So although most nutritional yeast is essentially cooked, there are still a few companies that still do it the old freezer way. Some companies also add things to their product. They are always listed, so just read the label.

Nuts and nut butters. There is a huge question about how nuts and seeds are dried. Many seeds such as sesame are hulled using steam. Some places, however, still use a machine for hulling. Nuts must be dried before selling, and many companies dry them in kilns and ovens at well over 200°F. Nut butters that are made from "raw" nuts are sold as raw even if the nut butter–making equipment heated the ingredients to well over 200°F. Truly raw nuts are usually freeze-dried.

Sea salt/Celtic sea salt. Watch out for iodized salts and kiln-dried mineral salts. Sun-dried salt is filled with vital nutrients only found in the sea.

Spirulina. Most spirulina is freeze-dried. This breaks open the cell wall (due to water expansion), increases its digestibility, and makes the spirulina more absorbable. This freeze-drying process does destroy the life force (the ability to grow and create more life). A few companies still sun-dry their algae. However, freeze-dried foods are considered raw by most, and so is spirulina.

Young Thai coconuts. These raw coconuts imported fresh from Thailand are definitely *not* organic. These nuts have been treated with various chemicals, including formaldehyde and bleach, and are processed by machines.

Raw Tools

Kitchen tools are a blessing to the culinary-minded raw fooder. By having a wide range of tools to work with, you can create gourmet meals to live for. Knowing what kind of equipment is right for you can help you get the results you want in the kitchen. This chapter lists the common types of tools found in raw food kitchens. For some items, I suggest both types and brand names.

Utensils

Household kitchen utensils such as bowls, knives, cutting boards, countertops, spoons, spatulas, and so forth are made from a variety of substances in our modern age. Some are better than others.

GLASS: A very inert substance; great for bowls.

CERAMIC: Natural earthenware; very pure.

STAINLESS STEEL: Very durable and easy to clean.

PLASTIC: Can affect the flavor of food.

WOOD: Best material for all utensils; great for flavor.

ALUMINUM: Extremely toxic. Watch out!

Juicers

Juicers separate organic liquids from foods. Fruits, vegetables, soaked nuts, and sprouts can all be juiced. Juicing concentrates the food's nutrients while removing its fibers, thus providing us with more energy that's more readily absorbed by our bodies (meaning more energy from less food). Be sure to juice only organic or unsprayed foods since otherwise the juicing process will concentrate any pesticides or other chemicals along with the food's nutrients.

CENTRIFUGAL: Centrifugal or spinning juicers are juicers that have a spinning metal blade in their upper chamber that shreds and spins off juice. These are the most common juicers available on the market. They are often cheap, easy to clean, and compact. Two recommended brands are Miracle and Juice Man. These juicers lack in efficiency, though; they extract only 60 percent of the juice. (To improve this rate, try running the pulp through a second pass.) Centrifugal juicers also cause the juice to quickly oxidize, and the juice may require straining.

HOMOGENIZING: These juicers use the process of mastication to grind and press juice from its source, much like our own teeth. The Champion Juicer (my favorite) is one masticating juicer available today; it grinds its little teeth on a hub and presses the fruits, vegetables, nuts, or seeds up against a screen or blank plate. Any homogenizing juicer can masticate (homogenize) foods into paste or a pulp as well as juice them. Masticating juicers are 80 percent efficient and produce juice that is much slower to oxidize.

JUICE PRESSES: Juice presses are one of the most efficient ways to extract juice. A press ruptures the cells from within. The juice produced is barely oxidized, tastes the best, and has the longest shelf life and stability.

Automatic: The Norwalk juicer is an electric press, much like the hand press. This machine also comes with a built-in grinder attached to the side for mashing harder vegetables or grinding sprouted grains.

Citrus juicer: Used to press the juice out of citrus fruits.

Hand press: These presses are made from two-ton hydraulic car jacks and stainless-steel screws, plates, and bowls. The juicy pulp of fruits or veggies is placed in a cloth bag inside a bowl and the juice is then pressed out by pumping a jack. Harder vegetables must be ground before hand juicing.

Juice bag: This simple juicer is inexpensive and lightweight, making it perfect for travel. Shred hard vegetables or fruits (juicy fruits can just be cut and inserted whole), then place in a mesh sprout bag or cloth. Squeeze over a bowl to catch the juice. This juice has the slowest oxidation rate, but unfortunately the method isn't very efficient.

Screw presses: Available in manual and electric varieties, these have a spiral screw that presses against a screen, forcing foods through the top, squeezing the pulp and juice. A wheatgrass juicer is one type of screw press.

TRITURATING: A triturating juicer is one that uses two gears to grind and press foods for homogenizing. This process is very similar to mastication yet happens at a slower speed. Trituration provides juice that oxidizes very slowly and is 90 percent efficient or better.

Blenders

Blenders are used to grind food into liquids.

BLENDER CUP: A small jar that fits upside-down on the blender base, allowing you to blend smaller quantities at a time. Blender cups also allow for more torque per square inch, thereby resulting in creamier, smoother blends. Most blender bases (the blade and bottom) have a standard type of threading that will actually attach to any small-mouthed jar, such as an old nut butter or honey jar. (Some hardware stores even carry the right-sized jars new.) The jars can be filled up to three-quarters full and, once blending is complete, the original lid can be screwed back on for storage.

DUAL SPEED: A blender with high and low settings.

MULTISPEED: A blender that has a variety of speeds.

OSTERIZER: A common household blender that often has optional small blending jars that attach for small portions.

VITAMIX: A super-powered blender that can blend dry or wet ingredients and grind almost anything into a liquid. The carafe holds eight cups (most blenders hold five cups).

Sprouting Equipment

Sprouting can be accomplished in a number of ways. Having the tools that work with your lifestyle and kitchen makes it much easier to keep a continual sprout garden in your home.

BIOSTA: An easy-to-use multitiered sprouting system.

JARS: Half-gallon glass Ball or Mason jars are best.

LIDS: Look for plastic sprouting lids that screw on. They are sold online or at health food stores.

MISTAPONIC: An automatic sprouting system.

SCREEN: Use a nylon screen, which is cheap and easy to find. A piece of screen can be affixed to the top of the jar, allowing for drainage and airflow while hindering the invasion of outside during the sprouting process.

SOIL: Garden stores sell organic soil, or use soil from your yard.

TRAYS: Plastic trays are available at gardening stores.

Garnishing Tools

Garnishes add an element of beauty to any meal. Many master chefs from Asia can produce a huge array of garnishes using any type of food.

CARVING TOOLS: Small knives and curved blades used to cut fruits and veggies into shapes.

PASTRY BAG: Used to decorate cakes or write using icing.

SPIRALIZER: A tool for making long, thin, curly strips of vegetables—as thin as angel hair pasta.

ZESTER: A tool for making thin strips of citrus rind.

Food Processors

These tools are used to grind food into a powder or paste or just to mix.

CUISINART: This solid standard comes in a variety of sizes. This machine is a true workhorse.

GENERIC: Good for light grinding but breaks easily.

KRUPPS: Makes an excellent mini-processor.

Culturing

You can use the following tools to create an ideal environment for living bacteria.

HARSCH CROCK: An earthen jar with a water seal used for making sauerkraut, pickles, and kimchee.

SEED CHEEZE BAG: For separating curds and whey. A seed cheeze bag is an organic unbleached cloth bag or a silk screen bag that helps in the draining process. Alternatively, commercially sold nut milk bags, cheesecloth bags, or even paint-straining bags are commonly used to help extract the water (whey) from the culturing seed cheeze. Some people even use old T-shirts or straight cheesecloth or silk screen to press the liquid out of the cheeze.

TOFU PRESS: Used to press water out of soy tofu. It is available in Japanese cooking stores or some specialty culinary tool shops. It consists of a square box with a removable top and bottom and holes in the sides for drainage. The top slips into the box, allowing weight to be put upon the tofu, which helps to solidify it as it curds.

Dehydrators

These tools are used to remove water and dry food.

CABELA'S: A great dryer, with a glass front, digital timer, and varied settings. Powerful and efficient.

CERAMIC DRYING TRAY: A flat porcelain or ceramic dish for solar drying.

EXCALIBUR: A dryer with a variety of temperature settings, good for both home and commercial applications.

HARVEST MAID: A large dryer good for home use.

STACK: Not very efficient, but a type of cheap and easy-to-obtain dehydrator. It stacks one tray on top of another, and has a heating element at its base, so this method relies on thermal convection for the drying process.

Raw Techniques

The basic skills discussed in this chapter are the foundation of raw food preparation. Although some of these techniques will take some time to master, a general understanding of them will allow you to create divine delights.

Soaking Dates, Dried Fruits, and Nuts

Dried foods can be rehydrated to make them easier to use in recipes. To be used as sweeteners, dates often require soaking for an hour or so, then blending until smooth. It is important to remove the seeds from the dates before using them.

Nuts and seeds from many fruits can be soaked to make them blend up more smoothly. Seeds and nuts contain enzyme inhibitors that limit their digestibility. When we soak seeds and nuts for 15 minutes, we release up to 50 percent of the enzyme inhibitors. By soaking them for the correct amount of time (see the chart on page 22), we can release all of the enzyme inhibitors, making the seeds and nuts easier to assimilate. Sprouting a seed or nut will give it more of a watery and sweet taste, so sometimes soaked nuts are better in a recipe than fully sprouted ones. Do not use soaking water from seeds, since it contains all of the enzyme inhibitors we are removing. (The soaking water from fruits such as dates or sun-dried tomatoes, however, is excellent to use.)

Garnishing

Garnishing is the art of beautifying foods. There are almost limitless colors and shapes to work with, so use your creativity. There are many different tools, too. A vegetable peeler can be used to peel the skin of a tomato to produce a thin strip that can be rolled up to look like a rose. A sharp spoon can be used to sculpt root vegetables into many shapes. There are also standard garnishing tools such as the radish roser, which produces a rose shape out of a radish, and the tomato scooper, which perfectly removes the seeds from a tomato. The Japanese have discovered some of the most beautiful ways to garnish foods, and there are a variety of books on the subject. Garnishing foods enhances the presentation and adds to our enjoyment of food. Remember, eating is an experience, and each part of it—from the atmosphere to the taste, color, and garnish—plays a large part in the pleasure it provides.

Composting and Recycling

In today's world, it is ideal to walk as lightly as possible upon the Earth. We have learned that the Earth's resources are exhaustible and that pollution is damaging. By producing less waste, we help make the future brighter. Almost everything is recyclable; whether it is used again or broken down and made into something new, it still results in one less tree chopped down or one less chemical created. Composting is beautiful, as it both eliminates all organic waste in a conscious way and refertilizes the soil for future growth. Composting can be made easier by adding worms or bacterial starters to help it break down faster. A good book on composting is *Let It Rot!* by Stu Campbell.

Finding Raw Food in a Cooked City

In most urban environments, there are farmers' markets where local growers go to sell their crops. Checking online at localharvest.org often provides good leads. Also, search online under "Health Food," "Restaurants, Vegetarian," and even "Farms," "Fruit Stands," or "Farmers' Markets." Once you find the healthy stores, take a look at their bulletin boards and pick up any health or new age magazines they may have for free. These publications often have listings of everything from "fruit for sale" to "raw gatherings" and may also list restaurants. If all else fails, most supermarkets now have organic sections, so find the biggest one you can and make do with their commercially grown "organic" produce. Metropolitan areas usually have a number of health food stores that serve different neighborhoods, as well as organic or health-conscious restaurants that serve some raw foods. Check out the Yellow Pages under "Health Food" or buy a copy of *The Tofu Tollbooth*, compiled by Elizabeth Zipern and Dar Williams, which lists just about all the health-friendly places in the United States, state by state.

Foraging in the Woods

Many wonderful plants found in the woods can be consumed. Almost every grass is edible, and some are very nutritious. Birch bark is edible; dandelion greens and flowers are edible. Most large fruits are edible. Many salad greens are available wild. It is a good idea to check out an herb and wild food guide for pictures of what each herb or green looks like. It is also helpful to contact native or indigenous people for more information about the edible plants in your area. Research is invaluable, because you want to be prepared when a life-giving plant comes into season.

Foraging around Town

Many people live in houses with fruiting trees planted in their yard. Amazingly, people often prefer to buy from a store rather than pick the fruit for themselves. If you see fruit falling on the ground in your neighborhood, consider knocking on the door or leaving a note asking whether it's okay to pick some of it. Many people will let you have all their fruit or will split the harvest with you.

Raw Travel Tips

When adventuring to new places, it can be challenging to find raw organic food. Many places in the world have become inundated with modern packaged foods, or their local denizens dine primarily on fast food and junk. Most modern cities do have some form of raw and organic resources available, yet sometimes we find ourselves in a dead food zone where there isn't any vital food available. In those situations, try to plan ahead or master the art of patience and fasting.

Airplanes

For airplane travel, it is best to bring your own food. This is the only way to ensure clean and fresh raw food. I've been told that a few airlines offer a raw option, and one airline offers only organic produce. These days it's challenging to get airline security to let you through without irradiating your food. If you happen to have food in your pockets, you can get a few things onboard without being irradiated. Otherwise, every bag goes through the X-ray machine. The amount of radiation is supposedly less than that emitted by a cell phone, yet this may just be safety propaganda. Personally, I either fast or bring what I can. One of the best travel foods is kimchee. When they break out the cart of microwaved beef, open up your kimchee. It will mask the smell of the airplane food and help build up good flora that airline radiation destroys.

Trains and Buses

On train and bus rides, it is easy to bring your own food. Certain whole foods travel better than others—avoid ones that can get squished. Prepared foods are great for this kind of travel as well.

Long Car Travel

Car travel gives you the best options of all. You can bring prepared foods for parts of the road trip and collect many fruits along the way. Each new destination becomes a new source of food and fun. Sprouts can also be grown inside cars or buses by hanging sprout bags from the windows. Some people have even created solar dehydrators in the back window of their car.

Hotels

Hotels are great for preparing food and growing sprouts. You can set up a mini-kitchen area with a cutting board and even set up a blender. The bathroom can be used as a sprouting area, and you can stock up the room with local produce.

Intention

As we think, so it is. Benjamin Franklin once said that he saw "more people get ill from what came out of their mouths than from what went in." This is to say that we are what we think and say as much as, if not more than, we are what we eat. Some of the most unhealthy food a person can eat is made by angry chefs or people who are upset. Love and positive intent can influence our creations as much as negativity and anger. By keeping a positive attitude while preparing food, we can add to the joy and experience people get when they eat.

Recipes

Food can be art. The best chefs are artists who combine visual appeal with flavor and texture. Once you know how to use the tools described in this book and discover which foods work well with each other, you can create dazzling dishes to delight the mouth and the eyes. All it takes is a little self-expression. These recipes are some fantastic discoveries that I have made. Remember to use your head, act with your heart, and follow your tongue.

Drinks

Almond Mylk	70	White Delight	79
Banalmond Mylk	70	Mellow Melon	79
Banana Mylk	71	Nut Bliss	80
Cashew Mylk	71	Sweet Lime and Aloe	80
Green Dream	72	Apple Zing	80
Storange Smooth	72	Nut Shake	81
Black Raspberry–Prickly Pear	74	Fire Water	81
Tangy Tango	74	Ginger Blast	82
Fruit Root	75	Iron Lion	82
Banaberry	75	Lilistar	82
Banacado	75	Tropical Ambrosia	83
Ruby Cooler (Sun Tea)	76	Thin Mint	83
Sprout Power	76	Soursop-Pineapple	83
Sunshine	77	Liver Cleanse	84
Coconut Milk	77	Rejuvelac	84
Green Clean	77	Intestinal Cleanse	85
Complementary	78	Flaxative	85
Freedom's Froth	78	Cooling Green	86
Nature's Nectar	78	eVe-8	86

Almond Mylk

I never really understood the concept of humans drinking milk from a cow. Cow's milk is designed to take an eighty-pound calf and turn it into a three-hundred pound heifer in a few months. Almond Mylk has more nutrition than cow's milk and is far more absorbable into the human body. Sproutable almonds are also a great source of proteins and amino acids. SERVES 1 OR 2

3 dates, seeded

3 cups filtered water

1/2 cup sprouted almonds (see page 20)

Place the dates in a small bowl, cover with the water, and soak for about 1 hour, or until soft. Transfer the dates and their soaking water to a blender, add the almonds, and blend until smooth. Strain through a wire-mesh strainer into a tall glass and serve. (The pulp can be blended again for a lighter batch or used for "rawies," or dehydrated cookies.)

Banalmond Mylk

This power-packed drink is great for providing extra energy. It's a favorite of a body-building couple I know. They say it goes right to their muscles. As a variation, blend in 2 teaspoons of raw carob powder. (Pictured on page 73, top center) SERVES 1 OR 2

4 dates, seeded

2 1/2 cups filtered water

1/2 cup sprouted almonds (see page 20)

1/2 vanilla bean

4 bananas, peeled, frozen, and thickly sliced

Place the dates in a small bowl, cover with 1/2 cup of the water, and soak for about 1 hour, or until soft. Place the sprouted almonds and the remaining 2 cups water in a blender and blend until smooth. Strain through a wire-mesh strainer, discarding the almond pulp. Return the almond mylk to the blender, add the dates along with their soaking water, and add the vanilla bean. Blend until smooth. Add the bananas and blend again until smooth. Pour into a tall glass and serve.

Banana Mylk

In Hawaii, banana trees grow everywhere; from seed, it takes only nine months to get a hundred-pound stalk of bananas. Bananas are excellent for making mylk as they provide a creamy texture and a sweet yet subtle flavor. There are hundreds of varieties of banana, but Williams and Bluefield work the best. As a flavoring variation, try any of the following: blend in 2 tablespoons raw carob powder; blend in the seeds of half a vanilla bean; blend in the seeds of half a vanilla bean and 2 tablespoons raw cacao. You can also first freeze the bananas and enjoy a banana mylk shake with or without any of the above variations. SERVES 2 TO 4

4 dates, seeded

1 cup filtered water, plus additional as needed

4 bananas, peeled

Place the dates in a small bowl, cover with the 1 cup water, and soak for about 1 hour, or until soft. Transfer the dates and their soaking water to a food processor and blend until smooth. Add the bananas and blend until creamy. If needed, add a little more water and pulse a few times until combined. Serve in a tall glass.

Cashew Mylk

This sweet and rich nut mylk is one of the most delicious and filling treats. Cashews blend up better than any other nut, so if you are looking for a really creamy consistency, use cashews. As a variation, blend in the seeds of half a vanilla bean or 3 tablespoons of raw carob along with the dates and nuts. SERVES 1 OR 2

2 dates, seeded

1/2 cup cashews

3 cups filtered water

Place the dates and cashews in a small bowl, cover with the water, and soak for about 1 hour, or until soft. Drain, reserving the liquid. Place the dates, nuts, and soaking liquid in a blender and blend until creamy. Pour into a tall glass and serve.

Green Dream

Spirulina, an ocean algae, contains more protein than any other food on the planet. I talk to people all the time who ask me where to get protein in a vegetarian diet. I always tell them that beef is about 25 percent protein; milk, 30 percent; soy beans, 35 percent; and spirulina, a whopping 70 percent protein! Besides its fabulous protein content, spirulina contains every vitamin and mineral. That's a lot of nutrition for one of the simplest single-celled life forms on earth. (Pictured opposite, far right) SERVES 2

4 dates, seeded

1¹/₂ cups filtered water

2 papayas, peeled, seeded, and chopped

1 cup coconut water

4 bananas, peeled, frozen, and thickly sliced

1 to 2 tablespoons spirulina powder

Place the dates in a small bowl, cover with the water, and soak for about 1 hour, or until soft. Transfer the dates and their soaking water to a blender and blend until smooth. Add the papayas and the coconut water and blend to combine. Add the frozen bananas and the spirulina and blend until smooth. Pour into a tall glass and serve.

Storange Smooth

This is a vitamin C-packed smoothie. Many people think of oranges as a great source of vitamin C. Although oranges do contain a fair amount of the vitamin, the top honors go to acerola cherries, hot chile peppers, and strawberries. (Pictured opposite, bottom center) SERVES 1 OR 2

¹/₂ cup hulled strawberries

2 cups freshly squeezed orange juice

2 bananas, peeled, frozen, and thickly sliced

Place all of the ingredients in a blender and blend until smooth. Serve in a tall glass.

Black Raspberry–Prickly Pear

Prickly pears grow prolifically in Hawaii and in the Southwestern United States. Many native tribes subsisted primarily on the fruit for almost one third of the year, while it was in season. The prickly pear is covered with hundreds of tiny thorns, so be careful when handling it. The barbed thorns are as small as fiberglass. Make certain to wipe down all cutting areas after preparing this fruit. (Pictured on page 73, far left) SERVES 2 TO 4

7 large prickly pears

10 black raspberries

1 cup filtered water or coconut water (optional)

To peel the prickly pears, make a 1/4-inch-deep lengthwise cut through the skins. Cut off both ends of the prickly pears and peel back the skins, removing the fruit. Discard the skins. Juice the prickly pears along with the raspberries in a juicer or purée in a blender and strain. Transfer to a pitcher, add the water if a thinner consistency is desired, stir to combine, and enjoy!

Tangy Tango

Kiwis are also known as Chinese gooseberries. There is actually a miniature strain of kiwis and a golden kiwi. All of them work great in this tasty and tangy smoothie. SERVES 1 OR 2

1 large papaya, peeled, seeded, and chopped

1/2 cup raspberries

1 kiwi, peeled and coarsely chopped

Juice of 1 large lime

4 bananas, peeled, frozen, and thickly sliced

1 1/2 cups filtered water

Place all of the ingredients in a blender and blend until smooth. Pour into a tall glass and serve.

Fruit Root

Combining the fruit of the tree and the root of the earth creates a tasty and well-balanced drink—the best of the earth and sky. SERVES 1 OR 2

6 apples, cored

6 carrots

Process both ingredients through a juicer into a bowl. Pour into a glass and serve.

Banaberry

This is your standard smoothie. All I can say is it is berry good. SERVES 1 OR 2

1/2 cup raspberries

1/2 cup hulled strawberries

2 bananas, peeled, frozen, and thickly sliced

1 to 2 cups fresh apple juice (2 to 4 apples) or filtered water

Place the raspberries, strawberries, and bananas in a blender. While continuing to blend, slowly add at least 1 cup and up to 2 cups of the apple juice, as needed, blending until smooth. Pour into a tall glass and serve.

Banacado

One day while traveling the road to Hana, on Maui, I had the pleasure of harvesting both a ripe stalk of bananas and some ripe avocados. Being hungry after a long drive, I began munching on the bananas when I noticed that one of the avocados had gotten squished. I started eating the mashed avocado along with the banana and discovered a delicious new combination. Later I found out that the banana-avocado combination is a Hawaiian tradition. SERVES 1 OR 2

2 dates, seeded

2 cups filtered water

4 bananas, peeled and thickly sliced

1/2 avocado, peeled and pitted

Place the dates in a small bowl, cover with the water, and soak for about 1 hour, or until soft. Drain, reserving the liquid. Place the bananas, avocado, and the reserved liquid in a blender and blend until combined. Add the dates and continue blending until a thick, smooth consistency is achieved. Serve in a tall glass.

Ruby Cooler (Sun Tea)

Sun tea uses concentrated sunlight to extract flavor and essence from herbs, fruits, and flowers. The pH of the water determines how fast it will extract the tea. The more alkaline the water, the faster it will extract the tea. SERVES 2 TO 4

1/3 cup dried hibiscus leaves

1/3 cup dried rose hips

6 cups filtered water

1/2 cup freshly squeezed lemon juice

1 cup freshly squeezed orange juice

1/2 cup pineapple juice (optional)

2 to 4 lemon or orange wedges, for garnish

Place the hibiscus leaves and rose hips in a large glass jar and cover with the water. Cover the top and set the jar in direct sunlight for 3 to 6 hours, until the taste is to your liking. Stir in the lemon, orange, and pineapple juices and refrigerate until chilled, about 2 hours. Serve in tall glasses, garnished with a wedge of lemon or orange.

Sprout Power

Sprouts contain some of the most abundant life forces on the planet—they're the potential energy of a whole plant. When given the opportunity to sprout, a seed will spend as much energy as possible to get a root in the earth and a leaf up to heaven. In doing so, a sprout creates more concentrated nutrition per ounce than it ever will in its entire life. Grow your own sprouts, following the simple directions on page 20.
SERVES 1 OR 2

4 medium tomatoes, cored

1 cup loosely packed sunflower sprouts (see page 20)

1/2 cup alfalfa sprouts (see page 20)

Juice of 1/2 lemon

1 teaspoon powdered kelp

1 teaspoon nutritional yeast (optional)

Process the tomatoes and the sprouts through a juicer into a bowl. Stir in the lemon juice, kelp, and yeast. Pour into a glass and serve.

Sunshine

This bright orange smoothie is a delight to the eyes as well as the taste buds. For a pumpkin pie–flavored variation, add pinches of ground cinnamon, nutmeg, and clove. SERVES 2 TO 4

7 apples, cored, or filtered water, as needed

4 persimmons, peeled and seeded

2 bananas, peeled, frozen, and thickly sliced

If using the apples, process through a juicer into a large measuring cup (you should have about 2 cups of juice). Place the persimmons and 1 cup of the apple juice in a blender and blend until smooth. Add the bananas and blend until smooth and creamy, adding the additional apple juice if needed. Pour into a glass and serve.

Coconut Milk

Coconuts have the bad reputation of being high in fat, but coconut water contains no fat, and coconut meat, depending on its maturity, can contain lots of healthy, good fats. It is amazing how much misinformation is out there. MAKES 1½ CUPS

½ cup fresh, finely chopped coconut meat (see page 50)

1 cup coconut water

Place both ingredients in a blender and blend until smooth. Strain. Pour into a glass and serve.

Green Clean

This green drink comes close to providing the nutrition and cleansing benefits of wheatgrass juice and is far tastier to drink. SERVES 1 OR 2

2 to 3 leaves kale

3 stalks celery

1 cucumber

½ cup loosely packed fresh flat-leaf parsley leaves

½ cup loosely packed watercress

Process all of the ingredients through a juicer into a bowl. Pour into a glass and serve.

Complementary

The look of this delicious smoothie determined its name. The drink's orange color is perfectly set off by the flecks of blue scattered throughout. SERVES 2 TO 4

1 mango, peeled and seeded

2 peaches, peeled and pitted

1/2 cup blueberries

4 bananas, peeled, frozen, and thickly sliced

2 cups freshly squeezed orange juice or coconut water

Place all the ingredients in a blender and blend until smooth. Pour into tall glasses and serve.

Freedom's Froth

When I first used to visit Hawaii I would stay with Freedom, who lives in the jungle of Maui. The Raw Experience was born out of ideas that Freedom and I tossed around back then. This drink was permanently on the menu as a tribute to him. SERVES 2

2 papayas, peeled, seeded, and chopped

4 bananas, peeled and thickly sliced

Juice of 2 small limes

1 to 2 cups coconut water or filtered water

Place the papayas, bananas, lime juice, and 1 cup of the coconut water in a blender and blend until combined. While continuing to blend, slowly add up to 1 cup of the remaining coconut water until smooth and thick. Pour into glasses and serve.

Nature's Nectar

This smoothie tastes like coconut cream pie. SERVES 1 OR 2

3 dates, seeded

2 cups filtered water

1 cup fresh, finely chopped coconut (see page 50)

Place the dates in a small bowl, cover with the water, and soak for about 1 hour, or until soft. Transfer the dates and their soaking water to a blender, add the coconut, and blend until smooth. Pour into a glass and serve.

White Delight

The vanilla sapote is misnamed since it is actually not a member of the sapote family but a member of the citrus family. Vanilla sapotes, also called white sapotes, are green on the outside with pale ivory flesh. The green sapote (a true sapote) is green on the outside and orange on the inside. Look for vanilla sapotes at Latin markets and specialty produce stores. SERVES 2 TO 4

8 apples, cored, or 3 cups filtered water

2 vanilla sapotes, seeded

1 large cherimoya, peeled and seeded

2 bananas, peeled, frozen, and cut into chunks

Seeds from 1/2 vanilla bean (optional)

If using the apples, process through a juicer into a large measuring cup (you should have about 3 cups). Place 2 1/2 cups of the apple juice and the sapotes, cherimoya, bananas, and vanilla in a blender and blend until smooth, adding the additional 1/2 cup apple juice if needed to create a soupy consistency. Pour into tall glasses and serve.

Mellow Melon

There are many ways to juice a watermelon, but my preference is to use a juice press, which keeps the liquid vital and prevents oxidation for up to twenty-four hours. When the juice oxidizes, it separates and forms sedimentary particles. If you obtain the juice any other way (centrifuging, masticating, or grinding), the juice will oxidize in less than one hour. It is amazing to see a glass of freshly pressed watermelon juice—it glows brightly, especially when put in the sun. (Pictured on page 190, top right) SERVES 2 TO 4

1 huge watermelon (8 to 10 pounds), rind removed and chopped

Place the watermelon in a juice press or in a cloth bag over a bowl and press or squeeze firmly. You can also blend the watermelon in a blender, slowly at first, then faster, then strain. Pour into tall glasses and serve.

Nut Bliss

This delightful combination of nut mylks and bananas makes for a thick, frozen shake reminiscent of an ice cream milk shake. SERVES 2 TO 4

Seeds from ¹/₂ vanilla bean

¹/₄ cup filtered water

1 cup Almond Mylk (page 70)

1 cup Coconut Milk (page 77)

4 bananas, peeled, frozen, and thickly sliced

4 seeded, soaked dates (see page 64), drained

Place the vanilla bean seeds and the water in a blender and blend until smooth. Add the mylk and coconut milk and blend to combine. Add the bananas and dates and blend until smooth. Pour into glasses and enjoy.

Sweet Lime and Aloe

Aloe vera leaves are a powerful intestinal cleanser, but the flesh is extremely bitter and often a challenge to eat. Citrus juice makes aloe much tastier. Look for cold-pressed aloe vera gel at health food stores. SERVES 2 TO 4

1 cup filtered water

1 tablespoon cold-pressed aloe vera gel

Juice of ¹/₂ lime

2 cups freshly squeezed orange juice

Place all of the ingredients in a blender and blend thoroughly. Pour into glasses and serve.

Apple Zing

This zippy drink is a delight to the taste buds. It is nice to juice the rind of the lemon through the juicer for an added spark of flavor. SERVES 1 OR 2

10 apples, cored

¹/₂-inch piece fresh ginger

¹/₃ of a lemon with rind, or juice of 1 lemon

Process the apples and ginger through a juicer into a bowl. Juice the lemon with rind, or stir in the lemon juice once the apples and ginger have been juiced. Pour into a glass and enjoy.

Nut Shake

When using frozen bananas, slice them up before putting them in the blender. This will ensure that all of the pieces blend up evenly, resulting in the most creamy "milk shake" imaginable. SERVES 1 OR 2

5 dates, seeded

2 ³/₄ cups filtered water

Seeds from ¹/₂ vanilla bean

¹/₂ cup sprouted almonds
(see page 20)

4 bananas, peeled, frozen, and
thickly sliced

Place the dates in a small bowl, cover with ³/₄ cup of the water, and soak for about 1 hour, or until soft. Place the dates, along with their soaking water, and the vanilla bean seeds in a blender and blend until smooth. Add the almonds and the remaining 2 cups water and blend until smooth. Add the bananas and continue blending until smooth. Pour into a glass and serve.

Fire Water

This is a great way to start a meal. Fire Water was served at The Raw Experience as a palate cleanser and digestive stimulant. It was a great opener to a meal at the restaurant and provided a new spin on stepping up to the bar and throwing down a shot. SERVES 8 TO 16

2 quarts filtered water

3 chiles (such as habanero,
jalapeño, or serrano, or a
combination for added flavor),
thinly sliced lengthwise

1 lemon, coarsely chopped

Juice of 1 orange

2 teaspoons beet powder
(see page 54)

Place all of the ingredients in a glass jar with a lid. Cover, shake well, and refrigerate for at least 2 hours or overnight. Pour into shot glasses, being careful to leave the chiles in the jar, and serve.

Ginger Blast

Ginger grows wild in riverbeds and the jungles throughout Maui. When hiking in the woods, the smell of fresh ginger is everywhere. Its wonderful scent and flavor enhance this bracing drink. SERVES 1 OR 2

1 pineapple, peeled, cored, and chopped

2- to 3-inch piece fresh ginger, peeled and minced (about ¼ cup)

½ cup filtered water

Juice of 2 lemons

Process the pineapple through a juicer into a large measuring cup (you should have about 2 cups). In a blender, thoroughly blend the ginger with the water. Strain through a wire-mesh sieve, discarding the ginger solids. In a pitcher, stir together the pineapple juice and lemon juice. Add the ginger water and stir to combine. Chill before serving.

Iron Lion

It is nice to make this root drink with dark red beets for a really earthy taste. Golden beets provide a far lighter flavor but are very nice as well. Beets are an excellent source of iron. SERVES 1 OR 2

8 carrots

1 beet, peeled

½ cup loosely packed fresh curly parsley leaves

Process the carrots, beet, and parsley through a juicer into a glass and serve.

Lilistar

Star fruit, or carambola, are a sweet juicy fruit with a very mild flavor. Mixing them with the juice of the passion fruit, which is sometimes known as lilikoi, brings out the tropical tang. SERVES 2 TO 4

5 star fruits, ribs removed and seeded

1 passion fruit, shell removed

Process the fruits through a juicer or purée in a blender and strain. Pour into glasses and serve.

Tropical Ambrosia

This piña colada–style smoothie is a delicious tropical drink. Pineapples are propagated by planting the top crown. A few years later, a new pineapple grows out of the center of the crown of the old one. SERVES 1 OR 2

1 pineapple, peeled, cored, and chopped

1 cup fresh, finely chopped coconut meat (see page 50)

4 bananas, peeled, frozen, and thickly sliced

Process the pineapple through a juicer into a large measuring cup (you should have about 2 cups). Reserve the pineapple flesh for making Fruit Rawies (page 102). Place the pineapple juice, coconut, and bananas in a blender and blend until smooth. Serve in a tall glass.

Thin Mint

This smoothie was inspired by everyone's favorite Girl Scout cookie. For a different treat, you can dehydrate this smoothie into rawies. SERVES 1 OR 2

6 dates, seeded

1¹/₂ cups filtered water

1 large sprig mint

3 tablespoons raw carob powder

1 cup Coconut Milk (page 77)

4 bananas, peeled, frozen, and thickly sliced

Place the dates in a small bowl, cover with the water, and soak for about 1 hour, or until soft. Place the dates and their soaking water in a blender, add the mint and carob powder, and blend until smooth. Blend in the coconut milk and the bananas until smooth. Pour into a tall glass and serve.

Soursop-Pineapple

Soursop skins are usually green, but if the soursop is allowed to fully mature in the tropics, it turns silver. Make certain to remove all soursop seeds since they are poisonous. SERVES 2 TO 4

1 soursop, peeled and seeded

1 pineapple, peeled, cored, and chopped

Process the fruits through a juicer into a bowl, pour into glasses, and enjoy.

Liver Cleanse

This drink is a great way to care for your liver, which filters the blood and eliminates many of the toxins the body encounters. This drink helps the liver remove old waste and also helps clear the gall bladder. This drink was called the "Elvis Parsley" on The Raw Experience menu because it made you shimmy and shake. SERVES 1 OR 2

¼ cup loosely packed fresh flat-leaf parsley

1 clove garlic

2 cups freshly squeezed orange juice

Juice of 1 lemon

1 tablespoon olive or flax oil

Pinch of cayenne pepper

Place the parsley, garlic, and 1 cup of the orange juice in a blender and blend. Strain through a wire-mesh sieve into a pitcher. Add the remaining 1 cup orange juice, the lemon juice, oil, and cayenne, and stir. Serve immediately.

Rejuvelac

Dr. Ann Wigmore, the woman who brought sprouts and wheatgrass to the world, was a major proponent of rejuvelac, a cultured grain drink full of healthy bacteria and enzymes helpful in the digestion of raw food (particularly when transitioning to a raw food diet). Drinking rejuvelac is also an excellent way to bring positive flora into the intestinal tract, thereby bringing the body into a more alkaline balance and strengthening the immune system. SERVES 2 TO 4

1 cup sprouted wheat berries or sprouted quinoa (see page 20), with sprouts of equal length as the seed

7 cups filtered water

Place the sprouts in a clean ½-gallon jug and add the water. Cover with a screen or leave open. Place the jug in a warm area, out of direct sunlight, and soak the sprouts overnight. Strain through a wire-mesh strainer, discarding the soaked wheat berries. The rejuvelac should smell slightly sour. Refrigerate until chilled before serving.

Intestinal Cleanse

Every once in a while, it is a good idea to help clear the intestines. Many people eat far more than needed or could have eaten better foods in their youth and are now ready to cleanse the unhealthy remains from their systems. Psyllium husks are the outer coating of the psyllium seed and they have a great ability to swell and help eliminate old intestinal mucoid matter that may be limiting the absorption of nutrients or impeding healthy digestive action. There are other bulking or brushing agents that work similarly, although psyllium is widely recommended and commonly available in most health food stores. This drink is a sweet and easy way toward better health. SERVES 1 OR 2

10 apples, cored
Juice of 1 lemon
1 tablespoon psyllium husks

Process the apples through a juicer into a bowl (you should have about 4 cups). Blend or stir in the lemon juice and psyllium. Pour into a glass and serve.

Flaxative

Flax seeds are a great source of fiber and can help to clean out the intestinal tract. This drink is a great way to help keep things moving. SERVES 1 OR 2

¼ cup flax seeds
1 cup filtered water (optional)
4 apples, cored
2 bananas, peeled, frozen, and thickly sliced

The flax seeds may be prepared in one of two ways: Place the flax seeds in a bowl, cover with the water, and soak for 15 minutes, until the seeds have absorbed all of the water and a gel is formed. Alternatively, grind the flax seeds into a powder using a coffee grinder or a small food processor. Process the apples through a juicer into a large measuring cup (you should have about 1½ cups). Place the flax and apple juice in a blender and blend until smooth. Add the bananas and blend again until smooth. Pour into a tall glass and serve.

Cooling Green

This light and juicy drink is satisfying and provides an abundance of minerals. Cucumbers contain much of their vital nutrients in their skin. Unfortunately, the flavor of a cucumber's skin is quite bitter. To enjoy a far tastier cucumber, skin included, follow these simple instructions: Cut the tips off the cucumber. Take the tip from one end and rub its exposed flesh in small circles on the skin near the opposite end until a milky white sap comes out of the skin. Repeat, using the other tip on the skin of the opposite end. Cut off the new ends now coated in white sap and use your new, improved cucumber. SERVES 1 OR 2

1 large cucumber

3 stalks celery

1 teaspoon powdered kelp

Process the cucumber and celery through a juicer into a bowl. Stir in the kelp. Pour into a glass and enjoy.

eVe-8

This flavorful drink combines eight vegetables and is power-packed with a wide range of nutrients that provide long-lasting energy. SERVES 1 OR 2

2 tomatoes

1 carrot

1 beet, peeled

1 yellow bell pepper

1 cucumber, ends trimmed and rubbed (see above)

2 stalks celery

$1/2$ cup loosely packed fresh flat-leaf parsley leaves

1 or 2 cloves garlic

1 or 2 shots of wheatgrass juice (optional)

Process all of the ingredients except the wheatgrass juice through a juicer into a bowl and stir to combine. Pour into a glass. Add a shot of wheatgrass to the glass for a lively kick!

Appetizers

Pesto Wraps	89
Flax-Dulse Chips	90
Corn Chips	90
Carrot–Pine Nut Dip	91
Celery and Almond Butter	91
Veggie Kabobs	92
Tofu-Stuffed Cherry Tomatoes	93
Mini Pizzas	94
Cabbage Rolls	96

Pesto Wraps

These delightful little treats were one of the many bite-sized creations that I came up with for a catering gig, and they became such a hit that people requested them forever after. SERVES 4 TO 6

3 large zucchini, peeled

Pinch of sun-dried sea salt

Juice of 1/2 lemon

PRESTO PESTO

2 cups chopped walnuts

2 cups loosely packed fresh green and purple basil leaves

3 cloves garlic

1 heaping tablespoon red miso

2 tomatoes, cubed

Chopped green and purple basil, for garnish

Using a vegetable peeler or mandoline, cut thin, wide strips lengthwise down the zucchini. Place the zucchini strips in a bowl, cover with water, add the sea salt and lemon juice, and soak for 2 hours, or until they taste clean (not starchy). Drain, rinse, and drain again.

To prepare the pesto, place the walnuts, basil leaves, and garlic in a homogenizer juicer or food processor and homogenize, creating an oily paste. Transfer the paste to a bowl and stir in the miso.

To prepare each wrap, lay a zucchini strip flat on your work surface. Drop a teaspoon of pesto in the center of the zucchini strip. Press a small piece of tomato into the pesto. Fold or roll up the zucchini strip. Secure the wrap by piercing it with a toothpick or place it, seam side down, on a serving plate. Serve garnished with the chopped basil.

Flax-Dulse Chips

Flax crackers are possibly the simplest chip or cracker to make and are a crunchy delight. All you will want is "just the flax, ma'am." SERVES 2 TO 4

3 cups flax seeds

4 cups filtered water

1/4 cup dulse flakes

Place the flax seeds in a bowl, cover with the water, and soak for 15 minutes. Mix in the dulse flakes. Drain through a wire-mesh sieve. Using one of the methods described on page 28, thinly spread the mixture 1/4 inch thick on the appropriate drying surface for the chosen method. Dry for 18 hours, or until crispy.

Corn Chips

Dehydration removes water while leaving the enzymes and nutrition of the dehydrated food intact. Drying corn concentrates its flavor, and drying the coconut makes it crunchy and oily, giving these corn chips great flavor and big crunch. SERVES 4

2 cups corn kernels (approximately 4 ears corn)

1 cup fresh, finely chopped young coconut meat (see page 50)

1/4 cup dried cilantro

Dash of freshly squeezed lime juice

Pinch of sun-dried sea salt

In a food processor, process the corn and the coconut meat until well combined. Add the cilantro, lime juice, and sea salt and continue to pulse a few times until chunky. Spread in a single sheet about 1/4 inch thick on a dehydrator sheet or on a flat piece of ceramic. Using one of the methods described on page 28, dehydrate the corn chip mixture for 5 hours, or until dry on top. Flip and continue to dry for 5 hours more. Cut into triangles and dry until crisp, about 2 hours more. Keep in a sealed bag or container to maintain crispness.

Carrot–Pine Nut Dip

Dips and spreads are a great way to start a meal. This creamy carrot dip keeps them coming back for more, so make a lot. SERVES 2 TO 4

4 carrots

2 cups pine nuts, soaked for 2 hours and drained (see page 64)

1/4 cup loosely packed fresh flat-leaf parsley

2 tablespoons loosely packed fresh cilantro leaves

3 tablespoons Bragg Liquid Aminos or nama shoyu

1 loaf Carrot-Almond Essence Bread (page 172), sliced, for serving

Process the carrots through a juicer into a large measuring cup (you should have about 1 cup of juice). Place all of the ingredients in a blender and blend until smooth. Pour into a bowl and serve alongside the Carrot-Almond Essence Bread.

Celery and Almond Butter

This was a standard snack in my school lunch and possibly the first recipe I ever learned to make. I never could get enough of them then, and I still can't now. SERVES 2 TO 4

1 bunch celery, separated into stalks and trimmed

1 cup sprouted almonds (see page 20) or raw almond butter

1/2 cup soaked raisins (see page 64), drained

Break the celery stalks in half and peel off any large strings. Cut the celery into 5-inch pieces. In a food processor, blend the almonds and raisins. Spread the almond mixture on the celery sticks and serve.

Veggie Kabobs

This dish has a high entertainment value. There is something to be said for fun food. These display beautifully and are almost as enjoyable to make as they are to eat.

SERVES 4

MARINADE

2 teaspoons olive oil

¼ cup Bragg Liquid Aminos

2 cups filtered water

2 tablespoons apple cider vinegar

1 clove garlic, pressed

Juice of ½ lemon

Pinch of paprika

Pinch of chile powder

Pinch of dried cilantro

10 cherry tomatoes

1 avocado, peeled, pitted, and cubed

1 onion, cubed and separated into thin squares

10 pitted olives

1 large red bell pepper, seeded and cut into chunks

1 small pineapple, peeled, cored, and cut into chunks

To prepare the marinade, in a large bowl, combine the olive oil, Braggs, water, vinegar, garlic, lemon juice, paprika, chile powder, and cilantro. Mix well.

To prepare the kabobs, spear the tomatoes, avocado, onion, olives, bell pepper, and pineapple onto 10-inch wooden skewers, alternating ingredients so that the tastes and colors mix.

Place the kabobs in a shallow bowl and pour the marinade over them. Marinate the kabobs for at least 1 hour and up to 10 hours before serving.

Tofu-Stuffed Cherry Tomatoes

Tofu is traditionally a live-cultured food composed mostly of a living bacteria known as Aspergillus oryzae. *Most companies pasteurize (cook) their tofu so it doesn't ferment too far, and in doing so kill all of its living cultures. A true unpasteurized tofu is a living food but not a raw food because it is grown on cooked soy beans. The tofu recipe below is for sprouted tofu that is both raw and live. Tofu takes time to master, so be patient.* SERVES 4 TO 6

BASIC TOFU

1 cup slightly sprouted soybeans (tail should just be poking out of the bean; see page 20)

2 to 4 tablespoons filtered water

1 teaspoon nigari

1 teaspoon miso

¼ cup diced yellow bell pepper

¼ cup minced onion, rinsed

1 clove garlic, pressed

2 tablespoons finely chopped fresh flat-leaf parsley

2 tablespoons finely chopped fresh cilantro

Juice of ½ lemon

Bragg Liquid Aminos

20 cherry tomatoes

2 teaspoons paprika, for garnish

To prepare the tofu, rinse the sprouted soy beans well. Using a food processor, grind the sprouted soy beans with just enough water to create a thick paste. Place the sprouted soy beans in a bowl and stir in the nigari and the miso. Cover the tofu with a piece of cheese-cloth. Place a second, smaller bowl inside the first, pressing so that it presses down on the tofu. (You may need to put a brick or jug of water in the second bowl to add weight.) Leave the tofu in a warm (70° to 85°F), dark place for 24 hours, or until it's dry and firm. Remove the tofu from the bowl and, using the cheese-cloth or a silk screen, squeeze out any remaining water.

In a large bowl, mix the tofu, bell pepper, onion, garlic, parsley, and cilantro. Stir well. Add the lemon juice and the Braggs to taste.

Scoop out the cherry tomatoes using a tomato corer or a sharp paring knife. Fill each tomato with a small amount of the tofu mixture and serve, garnished with the paprika.

Mini Pizzas

This may be one of the ultimate recipes in the world of raw cuisine. This mini-pizza recipe will convince anyone that raw food isn't just salads and nuts. SERVES 4

Pizza Crust (recipe follows)

1 cup Red Sauce (page 95)

1 cup White Sauce (page 95)

¹/₂ cup chopped fresh basil, for garnish

Beginning 1 day in advance, prepare the pizza crust.

To serve, place the pizza crusts on a tray. Spread ¹/₄ cup of the red sauce on top of each crust, then ¹/₄ cup of the white sauce. Garnish with the basil and serve.

PIZZA CRUST

MAKES DOUGH FOR 4 MINI PIZZAS

2 cups sprouted buckwheat or soft wheat, sprouted for 2 days (see page 20)

3 large carrots, plus 2 tablespoons shredded carrot

2 tablespoons shredded beet

2 tablespoons minced onion

¹/₄ cup flax seeds

2 tablespoons finely chopped fresh flat-leaf parsley

2 tablespoons finely chopped fresh cilantro

2 tablespoons finely chopped fresh basil

2 tablespoons nutritional yeast

2 tablespoons caraway seeds

2 tablespoons sun-dried sea salt

Homogenize the sprouted buckwheat with the whole carrots in a homogenizing juicer. In a bowl, mix the wheat mixture with the shredded carrot, beet, and onion. In a coffee grinder or small food processor, grind the flax seeds into a powder. Add the ground flax seeds, parsley, cilantro, and basil to the wheat-carrot mixture. Stir in the yeast and caraway seeds, and add salt to taste. Mix well (you may need to sink your hands into this one).

Using wet hands, press the dough into 3-inch disks, ¹/₄ to ¹/₂ inch thick. Using one of the methods described on page 28, dehydrate the crusts for about 12 hours, or until dry. To decrease the drying time, occasionally flip the crusts.

RED SAUCE

MAKES 3¹/₂ CUPS

7 dry-packed sun-dried tomatoes, soaked in water until soft and drained

2 large tomatoes, chopped

1 clove garlic

4 fresh basil leaves, chopped

2 tablespoons Bragg Liquid Aminos

2 tablespoons olive oil

1 tablespoon nutritional yeast

Place the sun-dried tomatoes, tomatoes, garlic, basil, Braggs, olive oil, and yeast in a blender, and blend well until smooth. The sauce should be very thick.

WHITE SAUCE

MAKES 3 CUPS

¹/₂ cup macadamia nuts

¹/₄ cup pine nuts

¹/₂ cup cashews

1 cup filtered water, plus additional for thinning, if needed

2 tablespoons olive oil

1 tablespoon Bragg Liquid Aminos

2 teaspoons nutritional yeast

Juice of 1 lemon

Place the macadamia nuts, pine nuts, and cashews in a bowl, cover with the water, and soak for 2 to 6 hours, until smooth and creamy. Drain. Place all of the ingredients in a blender and blend until smooth, adding additional water, if needed, to obtain a creamy consistency.

Cabbage Rolls

Cabbage provides some of the more durable leaves in the vegetable kingdom. Cabbage leaves can be used as a salad bowl, as a burrito "tortilla," or, in this case, as the wrap for cabbage rolls. This Asian-style dish was modeled after a Chinese cabbage roll that I used to eat after kung fu class. Sea palm is generally available in a dried form and must be moistened for easier digestion and culinary use. SERVES 4

8 sturdy cabbage leaves

¹/₂ cup sprouted mung beans (see page 20)

1 cup shredded red cabbage

1 cup shredded napa cabbage

¹/₂ cup shredded carrots

¹/₄ cup sea palm (wet)

2 tablespoons white sesame seeds

Juice of 1 large lemon

1 teaspoon mirin or rice wine vinegar

1 teaspoon sesame oil

1 teaspoon Bragg Liquid Aminos or nama shoyu

1 teaspoon raw tahini or pumpkin-seed butter

Place the cabbage leaves on a plate and place in the refrigerator (this will help soften them for rolling).

In a large bowl, combine the mung sprouts, shredded cabbages, and carrots and mix well. Add the sea palm and sesame seeds and mix well. Place the lemon juice, mirin, sesame oil, Braggs, and tahini in a blender and blend well. Pour the lemon juice mixture into the bowl containing the shredded cabbage and toss to combine. Cover and refrigerate for 2 hours before assembling the rolls.

To prepare each roll, fill a whole cabbage leave with ¹/₂ cup of the shredded cabbage mixture. Fold the ends in tightly to enclose the filling, then finish by rolling up the leaf in the opposite direction (like a burrito). If needed, pierce the rolls with a toothpick to keep them closed. Repeat for the remaining rolls and serve.

Fruit Dishes

Exotic Fruit Salad	98
Tropical Fruit Salad	99
Mixed Melon Ball Salad	100
Apples with Ginger Chutney	100
Star Fruit and Raspberry-Nut Kreme	102
Fruit Rawies	102
Apple-Cinnamon Cup	103
Cinnamon-Apple Sprouted Wheat	103
Persimmon Sunburst	104
Mango Bliss	104
Applesauce	105
Cherimoya Freeze	105
Banalmond Bliss	106
Pineapple-Pepper Salad	106
Pineapple-Ginger Pudding	107
Mango Pudding	107
Banana-Date Pudding	108
Papaya Fundae	109
Fabulous Fig Parfaits	110

Exotic Fruit Salad

Nature provides such a wide range of flavors and colors, and each area of the world has its own unique offerings. Travelers can take in more than just the sights of a foreign land; they can experience new tastes that broaden the senses. At home, look for tropical fruits in local Mexican or Asian markets. Poha berries are also known as Chinese lanterns, inca berries, golden berries, or psylis fruits; they are available at many markets in both fresh and dried forms, and the fresh ones are contained in a little paper lantern (hence the name) much like a miniature tomatillo. For a fun presentation of this salad, serve it in papaya boats—halved papayas with seeds and flesh removed. SERVES 2 TO 4

2 cherimoyas, peeled, seeded, and sliced

1 papaya, peeled, seeded, and diced

1 mango, peeled, seeded, and diced

1 eggfruit, peeled, seeded, and thinly sliced lengthwise

1 sapote, pulp seeded and mashed

5 to 10 Surinam (*pitanga*) cherries, pitted, or poha berries

Freshly shredded coconut, for garnish

Combine the cherimoyas, papaya, mango, eggfruit, and sapote in a large serving bowl. Gently fold in the cherries, sprinkle the coconut on top, and serve.

Tropical Fruit Salad

Tropical treats can add delicious new flavors as well as varied nutrients to your diet. Many of the tropical fruits in this salad can be obtained in Asian markets. If you live in the tropics, remove the seeds from the papayas, persimmons, and cherimoya, and plant them. In time, you'll be able to harvest and enjoy your own fruit. SERVES 4 TO 6

2 papayas, peeled, seeded, and cut into $1/2$-inch cubes

2 mangos, peeled, seeded, and cut into $1/2$-inch cubes

1 pineapple, peeled, cored, and cut into $1/2$-inch cubes

3 Hachiya persimmons, seeded and cut into $1/2$-inch cubes

1 cherimoya, peeled, seeded, and separated into small sections

1 small bunch bananas, peeled and thickly sliced crosswise

1 star fruit, peeled and thinly sliced crosswise

1 kiwi, peeled and thinly sliced

Freshly shredded coconut, for garnish

Place the papayas, mangos, pineapple, persimmons, cherimoya, and bananas in a large serving bowl. Alternate star fruit and kiwi slices in a spiral over the top. Garnish with the coconut.

Mixed Melon Ball Salad

This dish entertains not only with its delicious flavors but also with its shapes and colors. For a festive presentation, serve this salad in a hollowed-out watermelon. (Pictured opposite) SERVES 4 TO 6

1 cantaloupe, halved and seeded

1 honeydew melon, halved and seeded

1 watermelon, halved

Juice of 2 limes

Scoop out the flesh of the melons with a melon baller, place in a large serving bowl, and mix gently. Splash with the lime juice and serve.

Apples with Ginger Chutney

Apples are available year-round and make excellent "chips." By thinly slicing the apple lengthwise around the core, you can obtain an average of ten slices per apple. SERVES 2 TO 4

10 dates, seeded

3/4 cup filtered water

1 1/2-inch piece fresh ginger

1/4 cup freshly squeezed orange juice

Pinch of ground cinnamon

4 crisp apples, cored and thinly sliced

Place the dates in a small bowl, cover with the water, and soak for about 1 hour, or until soft. Finely grate the ginger with a ginger grater or fine grater to extract its juice (you should have about 1 tablespoon). Place the dates and their soaking water along with the ginger and orange juices and cinnamon in a blender and blend until smooth. Arrange the apple slices on a plate and pour the date mixture over them, or serve the date mixture in a bowl with the apple slices around it.

Star Fruit and Raspberry-Nut Kreme

Star fruit, also known as carambola, has five to seven deep lengthwise ribs that form beautiful star shapes when the fruit is sliced crosswise. The edges (points of the star) can be tougher than the rest of the fruit, so it is often nice to remove the edges and the seeds before use. SERVES 2 TO 4

1 cup dates, seeded

1 cup filtered water

1 cup sprouted nuts
(see page 20)

10 raspberries

2 star fruits, thickly
sliced crosswise

Fresh mint leaves, for garnish

Place the dates in a small bowl, cover with the water, and soak for about 1 hour, or until soft. Drain, reserving the liquid. Place the dates, nuts, and raspberries in a blender and blend slowly, adding the reserved liquid as needed until the mixture becomes smooth. Arrange the star fruit on a plate. Spoon some of the nut kreme on each slice. Garnish with the mint leaves.

Fruit Rawies

These delicious dehydrator delights are quick and easy to make. These were originally called "fruit cookies," but since there is no cooking involved, I've dubbed them "rawies." SERVES 3 TO 4

10 seeded, soaked dates
(see page 64), drained

6 bananas, peeled and
halved crosswise

1 cup peeled, cored, and
coarsely chopped pineapple or
4 apples, peeled and cored

1 cup chopped walnuts

1 teaspoon ground cinnamon

Dash of pure vanilla extract

In a food processor, blend the dates, bananas, pineapple, walnuts, cinnamon, and vanilla until the fruit is just slightly chunky. Form the mixture into little balls, using 2 to 3 tablespoons for each, and flatten each ball into a disk 1 inch thick. Arrange on drying trays and, using one of the methods described on page 28, dehydrate for 18 hours, or until dry.

Apple-Cinnamon Cup

This dish was inspired by harosset, a traditional dish made of apples, walnuts, and wine eaten at Passover. Whenever I go to a Passover seder, I bring this dish, and it's always a big hit. SERVES 2 TO 4

6 seeded, soaked dates (see page 64), drained

Juice of $1/2$ lemon

1 teaspoon ground cinnamon

1 teaspoon ground allspice

1 teaspoon freshly ground nutmeg

3 crisp apples (such as Fuji or Gala), peeled, cored, and shredded or cut into matchstick-size pieces

$1/4$ cup soaked raisins (see page 64), drained

2 tablespoons chopped walnuts, for garnish

In a food processor, combine the dates, lemon juice, cinnamon, allspice, and nutmeg and process until smooth. Transfer to a large bowl and stir in the apples and raisins. Spoon the apple mixture into individual bowls or ramekins, garnish with the chopped walnuts, and serve.

Cinnamon-Apple Sprouted Wheat

Sprouted wheat, a fantastic source of protein, still contains some gluten. It can be replaced here with sprouted buckwheat, which is gluten free and even higher in protein. SERVES 2 TO 4

8 seeded, soaked dates (see page 64), drained

2 cups sprouted wheat berries (see page 20)

2 apples, peeled, cored, and shredded

1 teaspoon ground cinnamon

1 teaspoon freshly ground nutmeg

$1/2$ cup raisins, for garnish

In a food processor, combine the dates, wheat berries, apples, cinnamon, and nutmeg and pulse until combined but still chunky. Transfer to a bowl, garnish with the raisins, and serve.

Persimmon Sunburst

Hachiya persimmons, also known as Japanese persimmons, are very high in tannic acid and taste like very bitter chalk when underripe. To avoid this, make certain that your persimmons are fully ripe and soft. The skin should peel off the fruit easily if totally ripe. SERVES 2 TO 4

6 dates, seeded
½ cup filtered water
½ cup fresh blueberries
4 ripe Hachiya persimmons

Place the dates in a small bowl, cover with the water, and soak for about 1 hour, or until soft. In a food processor, combine the dates, their soaking water, and the blueberries and process until smooth.

Starting at the point of each persimmon, slice an X shape through the skin, cutting all the way down to the nub on top. Place the fruit, point up, on serving plates. Gently peel the skin away from each fruit, and leave it hanging like the petals of a flower. Using a melon baller or a small spoon, scoop out a piece of persimmon from the top of each open fruit. Spoon some of the blueberry sauce into the open persimmon points and drizzle more over the tops.

Mango Bliss

This recipe has provided joy and fun for everyone who has tried it. I find that simplicity is often best. Besides, who could improve upon the mango? DELIGHTS 1

Mango tree
Ladder (optional)

Pick a ripe mango from the tree. Peel and eat it immediately, preferably on the beach or near a river.
Bliss.
Swim.
Wow.

Applesauce

Applesauce is a great treat for kids and a quick and easy side dish. As a variation, add 1¹/₂ teaspoons of ginger juice. SERVES 2 TO 4

¹/₄ cup raisins

³/₄ cup filtered water

Juice of ¹/₂ lemon

2 large, crisp apples, peeled, cored, and diced

Ground cinnamon, for garnish

Freshly ground nutmeg, for garnish

Place the raisins in a small bowl, cover with the water, and soak for 1 hour. Place the raisins, their soaking water, and the lemon juice in a blender and blend until smooth. Add the apples and blend until smooth. Sprinkle each serving with cinnamon and nutmeg.

Cherimoya Freeze

People throughout the South Pacific adore this dish. Many people in the Hawaiian Islands have told me it reminds them of childhood visits to local fruit stands where they'd enjoy a similar sticky, sweet frozen treat. When it is cherimoya season, I always make extra and fill my freezer. Serve with Buckies (page 205), with chopped nuts, or on its own. SERVES 2 TO 4

5 cherimoyas, peeled and seeded

Juice of 2 limes

Put the cherimoyas in a sealed container and freeze for about 8 hours, or until firm. Put the frozen fruit through a homogenizing juicer with the blank plate in place, or purée in a food processor until smooth. Add the lime juice and process until smooth. Pour into individual bowls and serve.

Banalmond Bliss

This creamy treat is an evolution of banana ice cream. As a frozen treat, this dish is pure bliss. Enjoy with Buckies (page 205) as an alternative to chopped nuts.
SERVES 2 TO 4

8 bananas, peeled and sliced

1/4 cup Almond Mylk (page 70)

2 tablespoons raw almond butter

1 teaspoon pure vanilla extract

Chopped walnuts, for garnish (optional)

Place the bananas in a sealed container and freeze for about 8 hours, or until firm. Put the frozen bananas through a homogenizing juicer with the blank plate in place, or purée in a food processor until smooth. In a large bowl, combine the almond mylk, almond butter, and vanilla. Add the frozen banana purée and stir until combined. Freeze, covered, for 1 hour, or until firm. Transfer to individual serving bowls, garnish with the walnuts, and serve.

Pineapple-Pepper Salad

Peppers give this recipe just the right crunch. Apple mint adds an especially nice flavor to this salad, but if you can't find it, any sort of fresh mint will do. SERVES 2 TO 4

1 large pineapple

2 red bell peppers, seeded and sliced

4 kiwis, peeled and thinly sliced crosswise

1/4 cup minced fresh flat-leaf parsley

1/4 cup minced apple mint leaves

Juice of 1/2 orange

With a sharp knife, carefully cut the pineapple in half lengthwise, remove and discard the core, and cut out the fruit, leaving 2 hollowed-out pineapple halves. Remove the abrasive brown eyes from the fruit. Dice the pineapple fruit.

In a large bowl, mix together the diced pineapple, peppers, kiwis, and herbs. Stir in the orange juice. To serve, divide the salad among the empty pineapple halves.

Pineapple-Ginger Pudding

Pineapples are the highest source of bromelain, an enzyme that breaks down protein. They are so high in these enzymes that they can be used as a digestive stimulant that helps ease gastric issues and aids digestion. SERVES 2 TO 4

10 dates, seeded

³/₄ cup filtered water

³/₄-inch piece fresh ginger

4 cups chopped, peeled pineapple

1 cup freshly squeezed lemon juice

Grated zest of 1 lemon

Coarsely ground almonds, for garnish

Place the dates in a small bowl, cover with the water, and soak for about 1 hour, or until soft. Drain, reserving the liquid. Finely grate the ginger with a ginger grater or fine grater to extract its juice (you should have 1¹/₂ teaspoons). Place the dates, pineapple, lemon juice and zest, and ginger juice in a blender and blend slowly, adding the reserved liquid as needed until the mixture is smooth yet thick. Pour the pudding into a decorative bowl, sprinkle the almonds over the top, and serve.

Mango Pudding

Mangos are among the most popular fruits in the world, and there are more than three hundred varieties. The fruit's avid fans have cultivated it all over the world, and people still breed new strains today. SERVES 2 TO 4

4 dates, seeded

¹/₂ cup filtered water

4 mangos, peeled, seeded, and quartered

4 bananas, peeled and halved crosswise

Freshly shredded coconut, for garnish

Place the dates in a small bowl, cover with the water, and soak for about 1 hour, or until soft. Drain, reserving the liquid. Place the mangos, bananas, dates, and ¹/₄ cup of the reserved liquid in a blender and purée. If needed, add additional reserved liquid until the mixture is smooth yet thick. Transfer to a serving bowl and refrigerate for 2 hours, or until well chilled. Garnish with the shredded coconut and serve.

Banana-Date Pudding

This dish was originally inspired by a banana-date-tofu pudding at an Asian vegetarian restaurant in New York City. I never did get the recipe for it, but this creation is an amazingly close raw version. SERVES 2 TO 4

6 dates, seeded

1/2 cup filtered water

Seeds from 1/4 of a split vanilla bean

6 bananas, peeled and halved crosswise

Chopped walnuts, for garnish

Shredded coconut, for garnish

Place the dates in a small bowl, cover with the water, and soak for about 1 hour, or until soft. In a food processor, blend the dates, their soaking water, and the vanilla seeds until smooth. Add the bananas and process until smooth. Spoon the pudding into individual serving bowls. Cover and refrigerate for 2 hours, or until chilled. Garnish with the chopped walnuts and coconut and serve.

Papaya Fundae

These "fundaes," always one of the most popular desserts at our restaurants, are a great party dish. SERVES 4

CAROB SAUCE

6 dates, seeded

$3/4$ cup filtered water

2 tablespoons olive oil or hemp seed oil

$1/4$ cup raw carob powder

BLACK RASPBERRY KREME

5 dates, seeded

$1/2$ cup filtered water

1 cup soaked cashews (see page 64), drained

$1/3$ cup black raspberries

8 bananas, peeled, frozen, and thickly sliced

2 papayas, halved and seeded

Chopped walnuts, for garnish

To prepare the sauce, place the dates in a small bowl, cover with the water, and soak for about 1 hour, or until soft. Drain, reserving the liquid. In a food processor, combine the dates and the oil, slowly adding the reserved liquid as needed until the mixture is smooth. Add the carob powder and pulse until combined.

To make the raspberry kreme, place the dates in a small bowl, cover with the water, and soak for about 1 hour, or until soft. Drain, reserving the liquid. Place the dates, cashews, and black raspberries in a blender and blend slowly, adding the reserved liquid as needed until the mixture becomes smooth.

Put the frozen bananas through a homogenizing juicer with a blank plate in place, or purée in a food processor until smooth. Fill the papaya halves with the puréed bananas, dividing equally. Top with 3 heaping tablespoons of the raspberry kreme. Drizzle the carob sauce over the papayas and raspberry kreme and garnish with the chopped walnuts.

Fabulous Fig Parfaits

Fresh figs are a wealth of life force, containing thousands of tiny seeds that make them a very virile and hormone-rich food. These delicate fruits are very popular in the cuisines of Europe and the Middle East, where they originated. Feel free to use any sprouted nut in the preparation of the nut kreme; pecans are just my favorite.

SERVES 2 TO 4

1/2 cup dates, seeded

1/2 cup filtered water, plus additional as needed

NUT KREME

1/2 cup soaked pecans (see page 64), drained

RASPBERRY SAUCE

1/4 cup raspberries

8 fresh figs

Mint leaves or freshly shredded coconut, for garnish

Place the dates in a small bowl, cover with the water, and soak for about 1 hour, or until soft. Drain, reserving the liquid.

To make the nut kreme, place the soaked nuts and half of the dates in a blender and blend slowly, adding up to 1/4 cup of the reserved soaking liquid, until the mixture is smooth yet thick.

To make the raspberry sauce, blend the remaining half of the dates, the raspberries, and the remaining 1/4 cup of the reserved liquid until smooth. The sauce should have a thin consistency; if needed, add additional filtered water.

To prepare the parfaits, starting from the top, cut the figs lengthwise into quarters (leaving the bottoms intact) and gently press open. Spoon some of the nut kreme into the middle of each fig. Arrange the parfaits on a platter and drizzle raspberry sauce over the top of each parfait. Garnish with the fresh mint leaves or shredded coconut.

Fruit Soups

Ginger-Pear Soup	112
Nectarine-Cardamom Soup	112
Fennel-Berry Soup	113
Watermelon Soup	113
Peach-Melon Soup	114
Persimmon Soup	115
Apple-Almond Soup	115
Berry Soup	115
Spicy Papaya-Lime Soup	116
Tropical Fruit Soup	116

Ginger-Pear Soup

The pear makes this soup—so be sure to pick a good one. When selecting pears for this dish, choose softer ones that are very ripe. I like to remove the skin before making this recipe as it yields a smoother consistency. To peel a ripe pear, just hold it under running water and rub the skin right off. SERVES 2 TO 4

6 dates, seeded

2 cups filtered water

1/4-inch piece fresh ginger

4 pears such as Bartlett, peeled

1/2 teaspoon ground cinnamon

2 fresh anise flowers, or 1/2 teaspoon anise seeds, or a few wisps of Florence fennel

2 mint leaves

Black and white sesame seeds, for garnish

Place the dates in a small bowl, cover with the water, and soak for about 1 hour, or until soft. Drain, reserving the liquid. Finely grate the ginger with a ginger grater or fine grater to extract its juice (you should have 1/2 teaspoon). Place the dates, pears, cinnamon, anise, mint, and ginger juice in a blender and blend slowly, adding the reserved liquid as needed, until smooth. Pour into bowls. Garnish with the black and white sesame seeds.

Nectarine-Cardamom Soup

With its cardamom and cashews, this summertime delight has an East Indian flair.
SERVES 2 TO 4

4 nectarines, pitted

2 teaspoons ground cardamom

1/2 cup soaked cashews (see page 64), drained

1 1/2 cups filtered water

Pinch of black sesame seeds, for garnish

Place the nectarines, cardamom, cashews, and water in a blender and blend until smooth. Pour into bowls, garnish with the sesame seeds, and serve.

Fennel-Berry Soup

In Kula, on the island of Maui, the Kula black raspberry grows. Wherever the raspberry grows, wild fennel grows as well. I would often rub my fingers on the fennel flowers and then pick the berries. The taste was fabulous, and that is how the flavor combination for this soup was created. SERVES 2 TO 4

3 cups raspberries

3 cups blueberries

2 tablespoons chopped fresh fennel fronds

2 cups filtered water

1 avocado, pitted and peeled

Fresh fennel fronds, for garnish

Place the berries in the blender with the chopped fennel and blend while slowly adding the water. Add the avocado and continue to blend until smooth. Pour into bowls, garnish with fennel fronds, and serve.

Watermelon Soup

A few years ago someone taught me a new technique for testing the ripeness of a watermelon: Set the watermelon on a table as it would sit on the ground. Take a dry straw from a broom, or a piece of hay, and lay it across the watermelon crosswise. The piece of straw will turn on its own toward the length of the watermelon. The more it turns, the riper the watermelon. SERVES 2 TO 4

8 cups peeled, chopped, and seeded watermelon, juices reserved

Juice of 1 lime

Filtered water, as needed

Place the watermelon in a sealable plastic container or plastic bag and place in the freezer for about 3 hours, or until very cold but not frozen. Transfer the watermelon to a blender, add the lime juice and the reserved watermelon juice, and blend until thin but still chunky. If needed, add water, $1/4$ cup at a time, until the thin and coarse consistency is reached. Transfer to a pitcher and freeze until well chilled, about 1 hour. Pour into bowls and serve.

Peach-Melon Soup

I had always been told that melons should either be eaten alone or left alone. In making melon soups, I've found that melons actually combine quite well with other foods—providing great taste and ease of digestion. SERVES 2

1 large cantaloupe, halved and seeded

2 peaches, pitted

1¹/₂ cups freshly squeezed orange juice

¹/₂ teaspoon freshly ground nutmeg

Using a metal spoon, scoop out the cantaloupe flesh, reserving half the flesh for another use. Set aside both cantaloupe bowls. Place the remaining half of the cantaloupe flesh, the peaches, orange juice, and nutmeg in a blender and blend until smooth. Divide the soup between the reserved cantaloupe bowls and serve.

Persimmon Soup

Persimmons typically become ripe early in the fall. Luckily, in Hawaii there is a springtime fruit that is a close relative of the persimmon: the chocolate pudding fruit (also known as the chocolate persimmon) or black sapote, which works great for this soup, too. SERVES 2 TO 4

5 persimmons, peeled and chopped

Pinch of ground cinnamon

1 cup filtered water

Place the persimmons, cinnamon, and water in a blender and blend until smooth. Pour into bowls and enjoy.

Apple-Almond Soup

This is a classic combo that tastes like apple pie in a bowl. If time allows, try sprouting the almonds, which makes for a less oily soup. SERVES 2 TO 4

2 apples, cored

1/2 cup soaked or sprouted almonds (see pages 64 and 20), drained

1 1/2 cups filtered water

1/2 teaspoon ground ginger

1/2 teaspoon ground cinnamon

Place the apples and almonds in a blender. While slowly adding the water, blend until smooth. Pour into bowls and sprinkle each serving with ginger and cinnamon.

Berry Soup

Any berry will work for this recipe. Blueberries produce a thicker soup, while raspberries and strawberries create a tangier, lighter soup. SERVES 2 TO 4

4 cups berries (such as blueberries, strawberries, or raspberries)

8 seeded, soaked dates (see page 64), drained

1 1/2 cups freshly squeezed orange juice

Place the berries and the dates in a food processor. While slowly adding the orange juice, blend until smooth. Cover and refrigerate until chilled, about 1 hour. Pour into bowls, serve, and enjoy.

Spicy Papaya-Lime Soup

Most of the papayas you'll find in the market today are hermaphrodites (half male, half female). These fruits are oblong and have a slight pear shape, unlike true female papayas, which are round and have five lobes. I prefer the flavor of true female papayas, but either kind will work fine in this dish. SERVES 2 TO 4

2 papayas, peeled, seeded, and chopped

Juice of 1 lime

Filtered water, as needed

Pinch of cayenne pepper

Place the papayas and lime juice in a blender and blend until smooth, adding a little water, if needed, to thin. Pour into bowls, sprinkle each serving with cayenne, and serve.

Tropical Fruit Soup

This island-inspired soup has a delightful tropical flavor that will make you feel the aloha spirit. SERVES 2 TO 4

$1/2$-inch piece fresh ginger

2 cups peeled, chopped pineapple

2 bananas, peeled and thickly sliced

2 papayas, peeled, seeded, and chopped

1 cup coconut water or fresh pineapple juice

Pinch of beet powder (see page 54)

Finely grate the ginger on a ginger grater or fine grater to extract its juice (you should have 1 teaspoon juice). Place the pineapple, bananas, papayas, and ginger juice in a blender. While slowly adding the coconut water, blend until smooth. Cover and refrigerate until chilled, 1 to 2 hours. To serve, pour into bowls and sprinkle each serving with beet powder.

Savory Soups

Creamy Carrot-Ginger Soup 118

Rosy Sea Soup 118

Tom Yum 120

Spirulina-Avocado Soup 120

Creamy Red Pepper Soup 121

Cascadilla Soup 121

Gazpacho 122

Maui Onion Gazpacho 123

Borscht 123

Cucumber-Dill Soup 124

Cream of Zucchini Soup 124

Corn Chowder 125

Curried Almond Soup 125

Almond-Onion-Parsley Soup 126

Cauliflower Chowder 126

Pesto Soup 127

Pea Soup 127

Cream of Broccoli Soup 128

Sweet Potato Soup 128

Creamy Carrot-Ginger Soup

This smooth and spicy soup was one of the most popular soups at The Raw Experience. (Pictured opposite) SERVES 4

½-inch piece fresh ginger

6 large carrots

1 avocado, peeled and pitted

2 tablespoons loosely packed fresh cilantro leaves

1 tablespoon Bragg Liquid Aminos

1⅓ cups White Sauce (page 95)

Black sesame seeds, for garnish

Finely grate the ginger on a ginger grater or fine grater to extract the juice (you should have about 1 teaspoon). Using a homogenizing juicer, homogenize the carrots (you should have about 2 cups).

Place the ginger and carrot juices, avocado, cilantro, and Braggs in a blender and blend until smooth. Pour the soup into individual serving bowls, top each with about ⅓ cup of the sauce, and garnish with the sesame seeds.

Rosy Sea Soup

Dulse is a purple North Atlantic sea vegetable that has a smooth and silky texture and is not overly salty. Dulse doesn't need to be soaked before use because it is so soft to begin with. Dulse is sold dried, whole, or as flakes. (Pictured opposite) SERVES 2 TO 4

1 beet

2 cups Almond Mylk (page 70)

½ cup dulse flakes

1 avocado, peeled and pitted

Bragg Liquid Aminos

Using a homogenizing juicer, homogenize the beet into a measuring cup (you should have about ¼ cup). Place the almond mylk, dulse, beet juice, and avocado in a blender and blend until smooth. Add the Braggs to taste. Pour into bowls and serve.

Tom Yum

This traditional Thai-style soup is my personal favorite. I love coconuts, and this soup is all about the coco. I like to use different ages of coconut meat to get varied textures. A more mature nut makes a chunky soup, while a younger one makes a creamy soup. I also like to use a variety of hot peppers: jalapeño, serrano, and even the super-spicy Thai chile, just to get a wide range of spiciness. Some peppers are hot as you eat them, others after you eat them; my favorites are hot only when you stop eating them. (Pictured on page 190, top left) SERVES 2 TO 4

1 coconut

7 leaves basil, plus additional for garnish

1 sprig oregano

5 sprigs cilantro, stemmed

½ Thai, jalapeño, or serrano chile, seeded and minced

2 tablespoons Bragg Liquid Aminos or nama shoyu

Open the coconut with a machete, cleaver, drill, or knife (see page 50). Pour the coconut water into a blender. With a metal spoon, scoop out the coconut meat and place in the blender with the coconut water. Add the basil, oregano, cilantro, chile, and Braggs and blend until smooth. Pour the soup into individual bowls and garnish each with a few basil leaves.

Spirulina-Avocado Soup

Spirulina offers a wealth of nutrition, providing an abundance of vitamins and minerals. This smooth and silky soup is packed with power and tastes great.
SERVES 2 TO 4

1 large avocado, peeled and pitted

1 cup filtered water

2 tablespoons chopped fresh cilantro, plus additional for garnish

2 tablespoons Bragg Liquid Aminos

2 teaspoons powdered spirulina

Juice of ½ lemon

Place the avocado, water, cilantro, Braggs, spirulina, and lemon juice in a blender and blend until smooth. Serve in bowls, garnished with additional cilantro.

Creamy Red Pepper Soup

This soup has a bright and sweet flavor that is well supported by the richness of the avocado. SERVES 2 TO 4

1 red bell pepper, seeded and chopped

1 avocado, peeled and pitted

2 cups filtered water

Leaves from 1 sprig oregano

2 tablespoons chopped fresh cilantro

2 tablespoons chopped fresh flat-leaf parsley

Bragg Liquid Aminos

Black sesame seeds, for garnish

Place the bell pepper, avocado, water, oregano, cilantro, and parsley in a blender and blend until smooth. Add the Braggs to taste. Pour into serving bowls and garnish with a few sprinkles of sesame seeds.

Cascadilla Soup

Cascadilla *means "cascade" or "waterfall" in Spanish, which is an accurate description of the outpouring of flavor from this sweet and tangy soup.* SERVES 2 TO 4

5 tomatoes

1 avocado, peeled and pitted

1 red bell pepper, seeded and chopped

1 cucumber, chopped

1 green onion, chopped

1 clove garlic, crushed

2 seeded, soaked dates (see page 64), drained

1 teaspoon chopped fresh dill

Bragg Liquid Aminos

Using a homogenizing juicer, homogenize the tomatoes (you should have about 4 cups of juice). Place the tomato juice and avocado in a blender and blend. Add the bell pepper, cucumber, onion, garlic, dates, and dill and blend well. Add the Braggs to taste. Pour into bowls and serve.

Gazpacho

Many people think of soup as something warm or hot. Yet in the heat of the summer, most people don't want a hot soup. Gazpacho is a delicious raw soup traditionally served chilled. This soup, which originated in the Andalusia region of southern Spain, is the basis for this amazing creation. SERVES 2 TO 4

2 large or 3 medium tomatoes, plus 2 cups diced tomatoes

1 small onion, minced and rinsed

1 cucumber, diced

2 green onions, chopped

Juice of 1 orange

Juice of 1 lemon

1 clove garlic, crushed

2 tablespoons apple cider vinegar

2 tablespoons olive oil or flax oil (optional)

1/3 cup coarsely chopped fresh flat-leaf parsley

1 teaspoon coarsely chopped fresh tarragon

1 teaspoon ground cumin

1/3 cup coarsely chopped fresh basil

1/3 cup coarsely chopped fresh cilantro

Pinch of cayenne pepper (optional)

Bragg Liquid Aminos or sun-dried sea salt

Juice the whole tomatoes using a juicer or purée them in a blender and strain. Set aside.

In a food processor, pulse the diced tomatoes, onion, cucumber, and green onions only a few times to mix and chop the ingredients, not to grind them. Place the reserved tomato juice, orange and lemon juices, garlic, vinegar, and oil in a blender. Add the parsley, tarragon, cumin, basil, cilantro, and cayenne and blend well. In a large bowl, combine the chopped vegetables with the blended soup. Add the Braggs to taste. Chill for about 2 hours before serving.

Maui Onion Gazpacho

The Maui onion is a special thing. It grows up at high elevations on the side of Haleakala crater. The onion is crisp and sweet, almost like an apple. In fact, there are people on Maui who eat them whole. Maui onions are what make this soup so good. If you don't have access to them, find a suitable sweet onion to replace it with.
SERVES 2 TO 4

3 large tomatoes, plus 1 tomato, chopped

1 Maui onion, diced (about ³/₄ cup) and rinsed

1 yellow or red bell pepper, seeded and coarsely chopped

1 clove garlic

1 cucumber, peeled and chopped

2 tablespoons chopped fresh dill

Juice of 1 lemon

1 to 2 cups filtered water

Bragg Liquid Aminos or sun-dried sea salt

Using a homogenizing juicer, homogenize the whole tomatoes (you should have approximately 2 cups). Place the onion, bell pepper, and garlic in a food processor and pulse a few times to blend slightly. Add the chopped tomato, cucumber, dill, lemon juice, tomato juice, and 1 cup of the water. Pulse a few more times, until thin but still chunky. If the soup is too thick, add up to 1 cup of the remaining water and pulse just once or twice to combine. Do not blend until smooth. Add the Braggs to taste. Serve immediately.

Borscht

This classic cabbage and beet soup is popular throughout Russia and the Slavic region of Europe. Borscht is hearty, healthy, and fun to say. SERVES 2 TO 4

2 to 3 cups chopped red cabbage

1 beet, peeled, shredded, and rinsed

2 tablespoons red miso

1 clove garlic

1 cup filtered water

Place the cabbage, beet, miso, garlic, and water in a blender and blend until smooth. Pour into bowls and serve.

Cucumber-Dill Soup

There is a cucumber called the lemon cucumber that is yellow and round instead of green and long. Lemon cucumbers add an extra flavor to this soup. If you can get them, use them; if not, regular cucumbers will work. SERVES 2 TO 4

1 cup sunflower sprouts
(see page 20)

2 cups filtered water

1 large cucumber, peeled and
chopped

2 tablespoons loosely packed
fresh dill, plus additional
for garnish

Pinch of nutritional yeast

Bragg Liquid Aminos

Place the sunflower sprouts and water in a blender and blend until smooth. Add the cucumber, dill, and yeast and blend until smooth. Add the Braggs to taste. Pour into bowls and serve, garnished with the additional dill.

Cream of Zucchini Soup

Creamy soups of any kind require some kind of fat to make them creamy. Avocado, soaked nuts, and coconut are the traditional raw sources. This recipe uses cashews, which, of all the nuts, provide the creamiest consistency. SERVES 2 TO 4

1/4 cup soaked cashews
(see page 64), drained

1/2 cup sprouted almonds
(see page 20)

2 large zucchini, chopped

2 tablespoons chopped
fresh cilantro

2 tablespoons chopped
fresh flat-leaf parsley

2 cups filtered water

Bragg Liquid Aminos

Dulse flakes, for garnish

Place the cashews and almond sprouts in a blender and blend until smooth. Add the zucchini, cilantro, parsley, and water and blend until smooth. Add the Braggs to taste. Serve in bowls, garnished with the dulse flakes.

Corn Chowder

On a visit to Georgia, a friend of mine turned me on to raw corn chowder. It was summer and corn was readily available, so each night we experimented with new evolutions of corn chowder. We decided this final version was the perfect chowder.
SERVES 2 TO 4

½ cup sprouted almonds (see page 20)

1 cup filtered water

1 clove garlic

¼ cup coarsely chopped fresh cilantro

2 large carrots, shredded

1 cup corn kernels (approximately 2 ears corn)

2 tablespoons chopped onion, rinsed

Pinch of nutritional yeast

Bragg Liquid Aminos

Place the almond sprouts, water, garlic and cilantro in a blender and blend until creamy. Add the carrots, corn, onion, and yeast and blend until chunky. Add the Braggs to taste. Pour into bowls and serve.

Curried Almond Soup

Many Indian restaurants in New York City use almonds in their cooking, and that was the original inspiration for this unique and delightful soup. SERVES 2 TO 4

6 carrots, plus shredded carrot, for garnish

2 cups sprouted almonds (see page 20)

1 cup filtered water

1 teaspoon turmeric

1 teaspoon Bragg Liquid Aminos

1 teaspoon ground cumin

1 teaspoon curry powder, or 1 curry leaf

1 teaspoon nutritional yeast

Using a homogenizing juicer, homogenize the whole carrots (you should have about 2 cups). Place the almonds and carrot juice in a blender and blend until smooth. Add the water, turmeric, Braggs, cumin, curry powder, and yeast and blend well. Serve in bowls garnished with the shredded carrot.

Almond-Onion-Parsley Soup

An almond can sprout only slightly at room temperature. For almonds to fully sprout and grow into a tree, they require a temperature of 57°F. Soaked and germinated almonds, however, still have a higher nutritional value than the original nut and are far tastier than a fully sprouted almond. SERVES 2 TO 4

1 tablespoon cumin seeds

½ cup sprouted almonds (see page 20)

2 cups filtered water

½ cup loosely packed fresh curly parsley leaves, plus ¼ cup chopped parsley, for garnish

1 teaspoon chopped fresh oregano

1 clove garlic, crushed

1 tablespoon olive oil

Bragg Liquid Aminos

⅓ cup minced sweet onion

Using a coffee grinder or small food processor, grind the cumin seeds into a powder. Place the almonds and water in a blender and blend until smooth. Add the ½ cup parsley leaves, oregano, ground cumin, garlic, and oil and blend until smooth. Add the Braggs to taste. Pour the soup into individual bowls, stir in the onion, and garnish with the chopped parsley.

Cauliflower Chowder

The cauliflower and almonds in this creamy soup create a synergistic combination that tastes something like cooked rice. This chowder is flavorful and fun. SERVES 2 TO 4

1 cup sprouted almonds (see page 20)

2 tablespoons shredded carrot

1 cup filtered water

2 tablespoons chopped onion, rinsed

1 head cauliflower, chopped (about 2 cups)

2 tablespoons nutritional yeast

Bragg Liquid Aminos

Place the almonds, carrot, and water in a blender and blend until smooth. Add the onion, cauliflower, and yeast and blend until creamy. Add the Braggs to taste. Pour into bowls and serve.

Pesto Soup

This Raw Experience creation has a robust flavor and chunky texture that make it "soupreme!" SERVES 2 TO 4

10 large fresh basil leaves

1 clove garlic

¼ cup pine nuts

1 tablespoon red miso

1 tablespoon nutritional yeast

2 cups filtered water

2 cups diced tomatoes
(about 4 tomatoes)

¼ cup diced red bell pepper

2 tablespoons shredded carrot

2 tablespoons shredded beet

2 tablespoons minced
onion, rinsed

1 tablespoon Bragg Liquid
Aminos

Basil flowers, for garnish

Place the basil, garlic, pine nuts, miso, and yeast in a blender and blend while gradually adding the water. Add the tomatoes, bell pepper, carrot, beet, onion, and Braggs and pulse until chunky. Serve in bowls, garnished with the basil flowers.

Pea Soup

Fresh peas are a fun summertime treat. Peas still in the pod are always the sweetest— plus they're fun to shuck. SERVES 2 TO 4

2 cups shelled fresh peas
(approximately 2 pounds
peas in their pods)

½ avocado, peeled and pitted

¼ cup loosely packed fresh
cilantro leaves, plus
additional for garnish

1 cup filtered water

Bragg Liquid Aminos

Place the peas, avocado, cilantro, and water in a blender and blend until smooth. Add the Braggs to taste. Serve in bowls, garnished with the additional cilantro.

Cream of Broccoli Soup

Broccoli and cauliflower are two of the most beautiful plants in nature. When flowering, these members of the Brassica *genus have giant bulbous flower heads surrounded by olive green, cabbagelike leaves. Broccoli stems can be used as well as the florets; just peel them first.* SERVES 2 TO 4

1 cup sprouted almonds (see page 20)

3 cups filtered water

1 small head broccoli, chopped (about 2 cups)

1/2 cup chopped red onion

1/4 cup loosely packed fresh flat-leaf parsley leaves

2 tablespoons nutritional yeast

1 tablespoon Bragg Liquid Aminos

2 tablespoons minced onion, for garnish

2 tablespoons chopped fresh cilantro, for garnish

Place the almonds and the water in a blender and blend until smooth. Pour the mixture into a bowl and stir in the broccoli, red onion, parsley, yeast, and Braggs. Spoon the soup into individual serving bowls. Top each with a little of the minced onion and cilantro and serve.

Sweet Potato Soup

To make sweet potatoes more palatable, after shredding them, soak them in water with some sea salt for at least 2 hours. This will help pull out some of the starchy taste and soften the potato for blending. SERVES 2 TO 4

2 sweet potatoes, peeled and shredded (about 2 cups)

1/8 cup sea salt

3 carrots

2 seeded, soaked dates (see page 64), drained

1/4 teaspoon ground cardamom

1 cup filtered water

Bragg Liquid Aminos

Place the sweet potatoes in a bowl, cover with water, add the salt, and soak for at least 2 hours. Drain. Using a homogenizing juicer, homogenize the carrots (you should have about 1 cup). Place the sweet potato and the carrot juice in a blender and blend. Add the dates, cardamom, and water and blend until creamy. Add the Braggs to taste and serve.

Salads

Mixed Field Greens with
Edible Flowers   130

Shredded Salad   130

Garden Salad   131

Zucchini-Squash Salad   131

Waldorf Salad   132

Corn, Carrot, and Pea Salad   133

Cucumber-Jicama Salad   133

Deluxe Salad   134

Sprout Salad   135

Little Italy Salad   137

Green Papaya Salad   138

Greek Salad   139

Sea Salad   140

Creamy Coleslaw   141

Root Slaw   142

Tabouli   144

Mixed Field Greens with Edible Flowers

Everywhere I go I find greens to eat. Wild greens grow without any cultivation or help. They have so much zest for life that they take over people's gardens. In the end, they just get insulted by being called weeds. I say, "Eat the weeds!" This salad is eater's choice. Use what you like; some greens are spicy, while others are bitter or sweet. Some edible flowers have a distinct flavor, while others are just there for color (see page 32). Be creative and design a salad that suits your tastes and is made of greens found in your area. Consult the list of greens listed on pages 37 and 38 for ideas. SERVES A FLEXIBLE AMOUNT OF PEOPLE

Greens of your choice

Edible flowers, for garnish

Salad dressing of your choice (see page 145), for drizzling

In a salad bowl, make a bed of greens. Garnish with the flowers, drizzle the dressing over the salad, and serve.

Shredded Salad

Quick to make and highly filling, salads of shredded vegetables are a welcome side dish to any meal. SERVES 2 TO 4

3 carrots, shredded

2 purple potatoes, shredded and rinsed

2 beets, peeled, shredded, and rinsed

2 cups shredded cabbage (about 1/2 head)

2 cups Carrot-Cashew-Ginger Dressing (page 151)

In a salad bowl, toss together the carrots, potatoes, beets, and cabbage. Drizzle the dressing on top and serve.

Garden Salad

This salad is standard fare in any restaurant. Nothing fancy, no frills, just your basic side salad. It's a quick and easy addition to a meal that needs just a little something extra. Make it with the freshest ingredients and it will be something special.
SERVES 2 TO 4

1 small head red leaf lettuce, torn into small pieces

1 small head green leaf lettuce, torn into small pieces

1 cup radish, clover, and sesame sprouts

1 cucumber, thinly sliced

2 large tomatoes, cored and cut into wedges

2 cups Green Goddess Dressing (page 148)

2 carrots, shredded

Pansy flowers, for garnish

In a salad bowl, make a bed of the lettuces and sprouts. Top with the cucumber and tomatoes and drizzle with the salad dressing. Garnish with the carrots and pansies and serve.

Zucchini-Squash Salad

Cucurbits such as summer squashes sometimes have a bitter taste to them. To improve their flavor considerably, soak the chopped zucchini and yellow squash in water with a pinch of salt and a dash of lemon juice, then rinse thoroughly. SERVES 2 TO 4

2 zucchini, cubed

2 yellow squash, cubed

1 onion, sliced and rinsed

1½ cups Almond-Cumin Dressing (page 146)

In a salad bowl, combine the zucchini, yellow squash, and onion. Drizzle the dressing on top and serve.

Waldorf Salad

The Waldorf salad was a popular dish originally created for the Waldorf Hotel in New York City. This raw evolution of the traditional salad is tastier than the original and offers a unique flavor combination. SERVES 2 TO 4

1 small Belgian endive, separated into leaves

1 large head red leaf lettuce

¼ cup peeled, shredded jicama

3 stalks celery, diced

1 apple, cored and diced

1 cup sunflower sprouts (see page 20)

½ cup chopped walnuts

1 cup red or green grapes

2 cups Waldorf Salad Dressing (page 146)

Arrange the five nicest endive leaves into the shape of a star around a salad bowl. By hand, tear the lettuce leaves into small pieces, then slice the remaining endive leaves crosswise. Mix together the sliced endive leaves and the torn lettuce and add to the salad bowl.

In another bowl, combine the jicama, celery, apple, and sprouts. Place the jicama mixture on top of the greens. Sprinkle the walnuts on top of the jicama mixture and the greens, then arrange the grapes on top to form a ring. Finish by drizzling the salad with the dressing. Serve immediately.

Corn, Carrot, and Pea Salad

This salad evolved from a cooked dish using frozen corn, carrots, and peas that I remember eating at summer camp. When I finally got around to making it, I was amazed at how much better it was than the original. Machine-processed, frozen, thawed, and cooked vegetables just don't compare to their fresh, natural counterparts.
SERVES 2 TO 4

2 cups corn kernels (approximately 4 ears corn)

4 carrots, shredded

1 cup shelled fresh peas (approximately 1 pound peas in their pods)

1 small onion, diced and rinsed

Combine all of the ingredients in a salad bowl, toss, and serve.

Cucumber-Jicama Salad

This cool and crisp salad is a great option when you want a lively texture. It has a good crunch and is fun to make. SERVES 2 TO 4

1 cucumber, sliced

1 small jicama, peeled and diced

1 apple, cored and diced

2 stalks celery, diced

2 cups Creamy Herb Dressing (page 147) or Cucumber-Dill Dressing (page 151)

Combine the cucumber, jicama, apple, and celery in a salad bowl and gently toss. Drizzle the dressing on top and serve.

Deluxe Salad

This was the standard salad at The Raw Experience. Many of the restaurant's recipes changed over the years, but this one stayed the same. If it ain't broke, don't fix it.

SERVES 2 TO 4

1 head romaine lettuce, torn into small pieces

1 head red oak lettuce, torn into small pieces

2 heaping tablespoons alfalfa sprouts

2 heaping tablespoons shredded carrot

2 heaping tablespoons shredded beet

½ avocado, peeled, pitted, and thinly sliced

2 tablespoons seeded, chopped yellow bell pepper

2 cups Carrot-Cashew-Ginger Dressing (page 151)

In a large salad bowl, make a bed of the lettuces and sprouts. Top with the carrot, beet, avocado, and bell pepper. Drizzle the dressing on top and serve.

Sprout Salad

There is no substitute for growing your own food. Having a daily interaction with the plants that ultimately provide you with food and nutrition is one of the greatest pleasures there is. Sprouts grow quickly and easily and can be grown in any season and in almost any situation (see page 20 for sprouting directions). I know people who grow sprouts while hiking, in their vehicle while traveling, as well as in their kitchen. Sunflower and buckwheat greens are grown in soil for a few days after being sprouted. This recipe is full of life force and packed with nutrients, and if you have grown the sprouts yourself, you can be certain that they will contain lots of your loving energy, too. SERVES 2 TO 4

1 tablespoon flax seeds

¼ cup filtered water

2 cups sunflower greens
(see page 20)

2 cups buckwheat greens
(see page 20)

½ cup alfalfa sprouts
(see page 20)

¼ cup wheat sprouts
(see page 20)

2 tablespoons sunflower sprouts
(see page 20)

2 tablespoons sesame sprouts
(see page 20)

2 cups Green Goddess Dressing
(page 148)

Place the flax seeds in a small bowl, cover with the water, and soak for 15 minutes, until the seeds have absorbed all of the water and a gel is formed. In a salad bowl, create a bed of the sunflower and buckwheat greens and alfalfa sprouts. Garnish with the wheat, sunflower, and sesame sprouts and soaked flax seeds. Drizzle the dressing over the salad and serve.

Little Italy Salad

This rich and aromatic salad—a classic from the kitchen at The Raw Experience—makes a hearty side dish. You can also serve it on a bed of greens and drizzle it with Italian Dressing (page 152). Marinated portobello mushrooms and sun-dried tomatoes lend a meaty flavor. The tomatoes and black olives also give a nice color contrast. SERVES 4

$^1/_2$ cup dry-packed sun-dried tomatoes (golden if available)

1 large portobello mushroom, stemmed and cut into $^1/_2$-inch pieces

2 tablespoons Bragg Liquid Aminos

1 small clove garlic, pressed

2 to 5 basil leaves, coarsely chopped

2 sprigs oregano, coarsely chopped

Juice of $^1/_2$ lemon

$^1/_4$ cup pitted olives, diced

2 tablespoons diced red bell pepper

2 tablespoons minced onion

2 tablespoons olive oil

Place the sun-dried tomatoes in a small bowl, cover with water, and soak for about 1 hour, or until soft. In another bowl, combine the portobello, Braggs, garlic, basil, oregano, and lemon juice. Cover and marinate for at least 1 hour. Drain the sun-dried tomatoes and slice them into small strips. In a separate bowl, combine the sun-dried tomatoes with the olives and bell pepper.

To keep their flavor from dominating, rinse the onions with water in a wire-mesh sieve. Drain the mushroom mixture, reserving the marinade for other uses. Add the onions and the mushroom mixture to the bowl containing the sun-dried tomatoes. Add the olive oil and stir to combine. If needed for additional flavor, add $^1/_4$ cup of the reserved marinade.

Green Papaya Salad

Island people all across the South Pacific, including Hawaii, eat green papaya salad. There are two fruits referred to as green papaya: one is a long, large papaya that doesn't ripen well and is only used green; the other is just a regular papaya that is used before it is ripe. Either may be used in this recipe. Green papaya has a much higher papain content than ripe papaya and therefore is even better as a digestive stimulant. Seeds of the green papaya, when dried and ground, make an excellent replacement for black pepper. Serve as is, or arrange on a bed of mixed greens and drizzle with Spicy Papaya-Lime Dressing (page 152). SERVES 4

2 green papayas, peeled and seeded

1 yellow bell pepper, seeded and diced

1 red bell pepper, seeded and diced

$1/2$ cup diced red onion, rinsed and drained

$1/4$-inch piece fresh ginger

2 tablespoons minced fresh curly parsley

2 cloves garlic, pressed

1 fresh jalapeño chile, minced

2 tablespoons olive oil

2 tablespoons apple cider vinegar

3 tablespoons Bragg Liquid Aminos

Juice of 1 lemon

Juice of 1 lime

Shred the papaya using a box grater or the shredding blade of a food processor. In a large bowl, combine the papaya, yellow and red bell peppers, and onion. Finely grate the ginger on a ginger grater or fine grater to extract its juice (you should have about $1/2$ teaspoon). Add the ginger juice to the papaya mixture along with the parsley, garlic, and jalapeño. Season with the olive oil, vinegar, Braggs, and the lemon and lime juices and serve.

Greek Salad

From the salsas of Mexico to the tapenade of Italy, and even to the green papaya salad of the South Pacific, every culture has something to offer the world of raw food cuisine. This salad borrows from Greece, whose cuisine features many traditional salads with cheese. This classic Greek salad utilizes seed cheeze in place of dairy cheese, and includes olives, another Grecian food staple. SERVES 4

1 head romaine lettuce

2 tomatoes, diced

2 cucumbers, diced

1/2 cup pitted and diced olives

1 tablespoon minced fresh oregano

1 tablespoon minced fresh basil

1 tablespoon flax oil

1 tablespoon Bragg Liquid Aminos

1 tablespoon apple cider vinegar

Juice of 1 lemon

1/4 cup Basic Seed Cheeze (page 166)

Tear the lettuce by hand into bite-size pieces and place in a large salad bowl. Add the tomatoes and cucumbers. In a separate bowl, mix the olives, oregano, basil, flax oil, Braggs, vinegar, and lemon juice. Add the olive mixture to the bowl containing the lettuce and toss. Serve with the seed cheeze on the side, or add the seed cheeze to the salad, toss lightly, and serve.

Sea Salad

This is a mineral-rich salad with an Asian flair. Sea vegetables such as seaweed are wild foods that grow in oceans throughout the world. If you can, get fresh sea vegetables that grow in your area. If that's not possible, then purchase dried ones. There is a large variety of seaweeds out there, so read the packages well and find one you like. Avoid sea veggies that are cooked before sun drying. Dried sea vegetables such as dulse, sea palm, and wakame are almost always dried fresh, while hijiki and arame are usually cooked first. Two good suppliers of raw sea vegetables are the Mendocino Sea Vegetable Company (www.seaweed.net) and Gold Mine Natural Food Co. (www.goldminenaturalfoods.com). Serve this dish on its own or on a bed of greens with Miso-Tahini Dressing (page 148). For individual servings, serve the salad on a large red cabbage leaf. SERVES 6 TO 8

1 large head red cabbage, shredded

1 large head napa cabbage, shredded

3 large carrots, shredded

2 green onions, thinly sliced

2 cups wet seaweed, rinsed and coarsely chopped, or 1 cup dried seaweed, soaked, drained, and chopped

Heaping 1/4 cup sesame seeds (white or black or a combination)

1-inch piece fresh ginger

3 tablespoons Bragg Liquid Aminos

2 tablespoons rice wine vinegar or white wine vinegar or other vinegar

Juice of 1 lemon

Juice of 1 orange

In a large bowl, toss together the red and napa cabbages. Add the carrots, green onions, seaweed, and 3 tablespoons of the sesame seeds and mix well. Finely grate the ginger on a ginger grater or fine grater to extract its juice (you should have about 2 teaspoons). Place the ginger juice in a small bowl and add the Braggs, vinegar, and lemon and orange juices and stir to combine. Drizzle over the cabbage mixture and toss well. Garnish with the remaining sesame seeds.

Creamy Coleslaw

Coleslaw has always been one of the great American picnic foods. This version's creamy consistency—the result of a special balance between its acids and oils—and its flavor of vinegar, tahini, and dates together enhanced by the mustard seeds, make it a slaw to remember. SERVES 4 TO 6

DRESSING

1/2 teaspoon dried mustard seeds

3 tablespoons raw tahini

2 teaspoons apple cider vinegar

1 teaspoon sun-dried sea salt

2 tablespoons nutritional yeast

2 seeded, soaked dates (see page 64), drained

1 large head red cabbage, shredded

1 large head savoy cabbage, shredded

3 carrots, shredded

To prepare the dressing, using a mortar and pestle, crush the mustard seeds into a fine powder. Combine the mustard seed powder, tahini, vinegar, salt, yeast, and dates in a blender and blend well.

In a large serving bowl, toss the red and savoy cabbages with the carrots. Drizzle the dressing over the top, toss well, and chill for 1 hour before serving.

Root Slaw

Shredded root vegetables of different colors make for a festive and bright salad. They also hold their color for a long time. Root vegetables are sturdy and can be carved and shaped in various ways to add flair and texture to a dish. Experiment with different styles of shredding and slicing to make this dish look unique. Look for the mirin in Japanese markets. Yacón is a sweet tuber grown in tropical environs. It has a sweet flavor almost resembling apples and is quite crisp like jicama, yet far more juicy. Yacón grows from the replanted root tops and the offshoots or tubers are harvested in the winter when the flowers die off. SERVES 4

1/4 jicama, peeled and shredded

1 beet, peeled and shredded

2 carrots, shredded

4 sunchokes, shredded (optional)

1/2 yacón, shredded (optional)

2 tablespoons nama shoyu or Bragg Liquid Aminos

2 tablespoons mirin

2 tablespoons flax oil

Juice of 1/2 lemon

1/2 teaspoon cumin seeds, ground

1/2 teaspoon mustard seeds, ground

1/2 teaspoon kelp powder

In a large serving bowl, combine the jicama, beet, carrots, sunchokes, and yacón. Combine the shoyu, mirin, flax oil, lemon juice, cumin and mustard seeds, and kelp powder in a blender and blend until smooth. Pour the mixture over the roots, toss well, and let sit for 1 hour, mixing every 10 to 15 minutes or so. Serve.

Tabouli

I was introduced to this traditional Middle Eastern vegetarian dish by the little gyro shops of the Lower East Side in New York City. Traditionally, tabouli is made from bulgur or crushed wheat. Sprouted quinoa has almost the same taste and a very similar consistency. I originally made this with ground sprouted wheat, but the whole sprouted quinoa has more life force (being whole) and is softer. The quinoa only needs to soak overnight and sit out and sprout for part of a day, and then it's ready to use. Black quinoa can be used for this dish for an exotic look. SERVES 4

3 cups sprouted quinoa (see page 20)

¼ cup olive or flax oil

1 teaspoon sun-dried sea salt

2 tomatoes, finely diced

½ large red onion, minced and rinsed

1 green onion, thinly sliced

1 red bell pepper, seeded and finely diced

½ yellow bell pepper, seeded and finely diced

2 or 3 sprigs mint, coarsely chopped

¼ cup minced fresh flat-leaf parsley

¼ cup minced fresh cilantro

Juice of 2 lemons

Mixed salad greens, for lining platter

In a bowl, mix the quinoa, oil, and sea salt. Stir well. Add in the tomatoes, onion, green onion, and red and yellow bell peppers. Mix in the mint, parsley, cilantro, and lemon juice and stir until the colors are mixed evenly throughout the dish. Serve on a bed of mixed salad greens.

Dressings

Waldorf Salad Dressing	146
Almond-Cumin Dressing	146
Creamy Herb Dressing	147
Sweet Mustard Dressing	147
Miso-Tahini Dressing	148
Green Goddess Dressing	148
Mango-Ginger Vinaigrette	149
Herbed Vinaigrette	149
Peanut-Curry Dressing	150
Avocado-Parsley Dressing	150
Carrot-Cashew-Ginger Dressing	151
Cucumber-Dill Dressing	151
Italian Dressing	152
Spicy Papaya-Lime Dressing	152

Waldorf Salad Dressing

This Waldorf-style dressing is a perfect replacement for the traditional mayonnaise-based dressing. It includes a great raw, vegan mayo replacement that is further enhanced with orange juice, dill, and onion, making an easy and delicious dressing for a Waldorf salad. MAKES 2¹/₂ CUPS

RAW MAYONNAISE

¹/₂ cup raw tahini

¹/₄ cup freshly squeezed
lemon juice

2 tablespoons apple cider
vinegar

2 seeded, soaked dates
(see page 64), drained

2 tablespoons Bragg Liquid
Aminos, or 1 teaspoon
sun-dried sea salt

¹/₄ cup freshly squeezed
orange juice

2 tablespoons dried dill

2 tablespoons minced onion

1 cup filtered water

Combine all of the mayonnaise ingredients in a blender and blend until smooth. Add the remaining ingredients and blend until combined. The dressing can be covered and refrigerated for up to 2 days.

Almond-Cumin Dressing

This simple dressing has a rich and robust flavor. Cumin seed is the dominant flavor, giving it an earthy taste. MAKES 1¹/₂ CUPS

¹/₂ cup sprouted almonds
(see page 20)

1 cup filtered water

2 teaspoons Bragg Liquid
Aminos

1 teaspoon ground cumin

Combine all of the ingredients in a blender or food processor and blend or pulse until smooth. The dressing can be covered and refrigerated for up to 2 days.

Creamy Herb Dressing

Avocados are the best thing to use to make a creamy dressing. It is important to choose a rich, fatty avocado, not a fruity, watery one. Sharwil and Haas avocados are both good choices. If you don't know the variety, it's often a challenge to tell what it will be like inside. Since there are more than three hundred varieties of avocado, it's best to try every type you can find, and once you find one you like, use the same type in all of the avocado dishes you like. MAKES 2 CUPS

1 avocado, peeled and pitted

2 tablespoons chopped fresh flat-leaf parsley

2 tablespoons chopped fresh cilantro

2 tablespoons chopped fresh basil

Dash of Bragg Liquid Aminos

1 cup filtered water

Combine all of the ingredients in a blender and blend until smooth. The dressing can be covered and refrigerated for up to 1 day.

Sweet Mustard Dressing

This dressing is spiced by the seed of the mustard plant and tempered by the sweetness of the carrot juice and dates. Using orange juice to replace the dates results in a tangier flavor. MAKES 1$^1/_2$ CUPS

4 carrots

3 seeded, soaked dates (see page 64), drained, or $^1/_2$ cup freshly squeezed orange juice

1 teaspoon ground mustard

2 tablespoons Bragg Liquid Aminos, or a pinch of sun-dried sea salt

1 tablespoon nutritional yeast

Process the carrots through a juicer into a bowl (you should have about 1$^1/_3$ cups). Combine the carrot juice and the remaining ingredients in a blender and blend until smooth. The dressing can be covered and refrigerated for up to 2 days.

Miso-Tahini Dressing

This Asian-style dressing was by far the most popular choice for salads at The Raw Experience. It is salty and creamy and seems to bathe the salad in a divine nectar. Well-aged (two years or longer) white miso is what gives the flavor to this dressing, and the tahini is what makes it creamy. MAKES 1½ CUPS

2 tablespoons raw tahini

2 heaping tablespoons white miso

1 seeded, soaked date (see page 64), drained

1 cup filtered water

Juice of 1 lemon

Combine all of the ingredients in a blender and blend until smooth. The dressing can be covered and refrigerated for up to 3 days.

Green Goddess Dressing

There are many dressings out there called "Green Goddess." This recipe was the version we served at The Raw Experience. I don't know what is in any of the other ones, but I do know that this was created out of my garden. It was composed from the gifts of the earth goddess, and since the dressing was green, I called it Green Goddess. MAKES 3 CUPS

1 cup sunflower sprouts (see page 20)

2 tablespoons chopped fresh curly parsley

2 tablespoons chopped fresh dill

2 tablespoons chopped fresh cilantro

Juice of 1 lemon

2 tablespoons Bragg Liquid Aminos

1 cup filtered water

Combine all of the ingredients in a blender and blend until smooth. The dressing can be covered and refrigerated for up to 1 day.

Mango-Ginger Vinaigrette

This Asian-style dressing is sweet and tangy. MAKES 2 CUPS

1 mango, peeled and seeded

3-inch piece fresh ginger, peeled and chopped

3 tablespoons apple cider vinegar

1 cup filtered water

Juice of 1 lemon

Combine all of the ingredients in a blender and blend well. The dressing can be covered and refrigerated for up to 4 days.

Herbed Vinaigrette

Centuries ago Europeans began scenting their oils and vinegars with herbs by leaving herb sprigs to sit in glass jars of oils and vinegars for months, or even years, to slowly extract the essence of the plant. This vinaigrette is a tribute to that tradition. If you like, keep the herbs whole and place all of the ingredients in a covered glass jar, leave it to sit in a cool place for a month or so, and then blend. MAKES ³/₄ CUP

¹/₄ cup olive oil

¹/₄ cup red wine vinegar or apple cider vinegar

2 tablespoons Bragg Liquid Aminos

1 clove garlic, crushed

3 sprigs flat-leaf parsley, chopped

4 sprigs dill, chopped

3 sprigs cilantro, chopped

Combine all of the ingredients in a blender or food processor and purée until smooth. The dressing can be covered and refrigerated for up to 4 days.

Peanut-Curry Dressing

From India to Thailand, curry is used in many cuisines. Curry powder is actually a mixture made of many spices from a variety of plants. Turmeric, ginger, ajowan, and other spices are all often used to make curry powder. There is also a curry tree that produces a very aromatic and spicy leaf that is a common ingredient in many Indian curry powders. MAKES 2½ CUPS

1 cup soaked peanuts (see page 64), drained

1 teaspoon curry powder

1 tablespoon Bragg Liquid Aminos

½-inch piece fresh ginger, peeled

1 cup filtered water

Combine all of the ingredients in a blender or food processor and blend or pulse until smooth. The dressing can be covered and refrigerated for up to 2 days.

Avocado-Parsley Dressing

This creamy dressing has both strong and subtle flavors. The parsley gives the dressing an herbal and earthy tone, while the lemon's acidity cuts through the fat of the avocado and offers a light yet smooth texture. MAKES 2 CUPS

1 avocado, peeled and pitted

½ cup loosely packed fresh flat-leaf parsley leaves

1 tablespoon Bragg Liquid Aminos

1 teaspoon ground cumin

Juice of ½ lemon

1 cup filtered water

Combine all of the ingredients in a blender or food processor and blend or pulse until smooth. The dressing can be covered and refrigerated for up to 1 day.

Carrot-Cashew-Ginger Dressing

This Raw Experience classic is zingy and creamy. Some people even eat it as a soup.
MAKES 2¹/₂ CUPS

6 carrots

1-inch piece fresh ginger

2 tablespoons soaked cashews (see page 64), drained

2 tablespoons Bragg Liquid Aminos

Process the carrots through a juicer into a large measuring cup (you should have approximately 2 cups). Reserve ¹/₄ cup of carrot pulp from juicing the carrots. Process the ginger through the juicer into the bowl of a food processor. Add the carrot juice and the cashews and process until smooth. Add the reserved carrot pulp and Braggs and pulse once or twice to combine. The dressing can be covered and refrigerated for up to 2 days.

Cucumber-Dill Dressing

This light dressing is perfect when you want the flavor of the salad to be stronger than that of the dressing. Its flavor is sweet and sour yet not overpowering. MAKES 2 CUPS

1 cucumber, thickly sliced

¹/₄ cup chopped fresh dill

1 tablespoon Bragg Liquid Aminos

Juice of ¹/₄ lemon

1 cup filtered water or cucumber juice (from about 2 cucumbers)

Combine all of the ingredients in a blender and blend until smooth. The dressing can be covered and refrigerated for up to 2 days.

Italian Dressing

The herbs used in this recipe are some of the easiest to grow at home. Fresh basil, oregano, cilantro, and parsley can all add true flavor to your meals. Each also produces a flavor that makes a beautiful garnish and helps bring out the subtler flavors.

MAKES 2¹/₂ CUPS

2 tablespoons chopped
fresh basil

2 tablespoons chopped
fresh oregano

2 tablespoons chopped
fresh flat-leaf parsley

Juice of 1 lemon

4 teaspoons apple cider vinegar

1 tablespoon olive oil

1 tablespoon Bragg Liquid
Aminos

¹/₂ cucumber, thickly sliced

1 tablespoon dried onion flakes

1 teaspoon paprika

1 cup filtered water

Combine all of the ingredients in a blender or food processor and blend or pulse until smooth. The dressing can be covered and refrigerated for up to 2 days.

Spicy Papaya-Lime Dressing

This traditional Hawaiian Island dressing has a fruity flavor with a real kick.

MAKES 3 CUPS

1 medium to large papaya,
peeled

Juice of 1 lime

1 tablespoon cayenne pepper

1 cup filtered water

2 to 3 tablespoons Bragg
Liquid Aminos

Seed the papaya, reserving 2 teaspoons of the seeds. Place the papaya, lime juice, cayenne, water, and reserved papaya seeds in a blender and blend until smooth. Add the Braggs to taste. The dressing can be covered and refrigerated for up to 3 days.

Sides

Kimchee	154
Traditional Guacamole	156
Star Fruit Guacamole	156
Star Fruit Salsa	157
Red Pepper–Chipotle Salsa	158
Tomatillo Salsa	159
Chile Mole	160
Pea Mole	161
Onion-Walnut Pâté	161
Cashew-Beet Pâté	162
Sunny Red Pepper Pâté	163
Carrot-Almond Pâté	164
Unstuffing	165
Cranberry Sauce	165
Basic Seed Cheeze	166
Festive Seed Cheeze	167
Pumpkin-Cashew Seed Cheeze	167
Rich and Creamy Seed Cheeze	168
Herbed Garlic Seed Cheeze	168
Colorful Tofu Salad	169
Tapenade	169
Essence Breads	170
Herbed Essence Bread	171
Apple-Cinnamon Essence Bread	171
Carrot-Almond Essence Bread	172
Fruit and Nut Essence Bread	172
Caraway-Onion Essence Bread	173
Pumpkin Butter	173
Baba Ghanoush	174
Sprouted Hummus	174

Kimchee

Kimchee is an Asian version of sauerkraut, or fermented cabbage. Kimchee has a tangy and spicy flavor; it is also considered a healing food because it helps bring healthy balance back to the intestinal flora. To start the culture, you'll need a tablespoon of prepared kimchee. Using some of a previous batch is best, but you can also purchase kimchee—just make sure it's "live" (unpasteurized) kimchee and doesn't contain any sugar or chemicals. SERVES 4

½ head red cabbage

½ head napa cabbage

1-inch piece fresh ginger

1 heaping tablespoon red miso

1 jalapeño chile, seeded and diced

1 tablespoon prepared kimchee

There are three different traditional styles of chopping the cabbage for this dish: (1) Thai style: shred the cabbage using either the shredding blade of a food processor or a hand shredder; (2) Korean style: slice the cabbage using the small slicing blade of a food processor or by hand using a sharp knife; (3) Hawaiian style: using a blender, homogenizing juicer, or food processor, grind the cabbage until it becomes mush. Using one method or some combination of the three, prepare the red cabbage and the napa cabbage. Place both cabbages in a large ceramic bowl or a traditional kimchee or sauerkraut crock, and toss.

In a homogenizing juicer, juice the ginger and ¼ cup, firmly packed, of the prepared cabbage. Place the juiced cabbage and ginger in a bowl, add the miso, jalapeño, and prepared kimchee, and stir well. Add this mixture to the tossed cabbage in the bowl and toss well to combine. Cover with a piece of cheesecloth. Place a second bowl of the same size on top of the first. (This second bowl will act as a weight.) Leave in a warm (75° to 90°F), dark location for 2 days. When your kimchee is ready, it will smell strong.

Traditional Guacamole

Avocados may be the most celebrated fruit in the world of raw foods. This traditional guacamole is a Mexican recipe handed down to me by my friend Josh. Roll the guacamole in lettuce leaves to make burritos, or serve with flax chips and sliced veggies for dipping. SERVES 4

2 very ripe avocados, peeled and pitted

1 large tomato, diced

¼ onion, diced

½ teaspoon sun-dried sea salt

2 tablespoons chopped fresh cilantro

Juice of ½ lemon

Pinch of nutritional yeast

Pinch of cumin

In a large bowl, mash the avocados. Add the remaining ingredients and stir well.

Star Fruit Guacamole

A giant star fruit tree behind the Maui Raw Experience inspired this delicious guacamole. Roll the guacamole in lettuce leaves to make burritos, or serve with flax chips and sliced veggies for dipping. SERVES 4

2 avocados, peeled and pitted

2 small star fruits, ribs removed and diced

1 tomatillo, diced

¼ cup diced shallot

1 tablespoon Bragg Liquid Aminos

Juice of 1 lemon

2 tablespoons chopped fresh cilantro

In a large bowl, mash the avocados. Add the remaining ingredients and stir well.

Star Fruit Salsa

One winter while vacationing on Maui, I created this fabulous salsa. I had an abundance of star fruits and was going to a potluck gathering. I had already tasted mango salsa and papaya salsa, both of which are Hawaiian specialties, so I decided to discover star fruit salsa. This sweet and tangy salsa was a huge hit and often appeared on the menu at The Raw Experience. Serve this salsa with Flax-Dulse Chips (page 90).

SERVES 4

5 star fruits, ribs removed and diced

1 cup pitted and diced olives

1 small onion, minced and rinsed

1½-inch piece fresh ginger

2 tablespoons minced fresh cilantro

1 tablespoon apple cider vinegar

1 clove garlic, crushed

2 tablespoons Bragg Liquid Aminos

Juice of 1 lemon

Bottom half of a jalapeño chile, seeded and minced

In a large bowl, combine the star fruits, olives, and onion. Finely grate the ginger on a ginger grater or fine grater to extract its juice (you should have about 1 tablespoon). Add the ginger juice, cilantro, vinegar, garlic, Braggs, lemon juice, and jalapeño to the star fruit mixture and mix well. Cover and let sit in the refrigerator or at room temperature for 1 to 4 hours, until the flavors mingle. Serve with flax chips.

Red Pepper–Chipotle Salsa

The chipotle chile (a dried and smoked jalapeño) has a robust and smoky flavor. Both black and red dried chipotles are sold; the red ones seem to have more flavor, but the black ones are far spicier. These chiles are available pickled and in adobo sauce, but only the dried chipotles are raw. SERVES 4

1 chipotle chile

5 dry-packed sun-dried tomatoes

2 red bell peppers, seeded and diced

1 large tomato, cubed

¼ cup diced onion

2 tablespoons minced fresh cilantro

2 leaves fresh basil

1 tablespoon olive oil

½ teaspoon sun-dried sea salt

Juice of ½ lemon

In a small bowl, soak the chipotle and sun-dried tomatoes in water to cover until soft. Drain. Mince the chipotle and sun-dried tomatoes and set aside. In a large bowl, mix the bell peppers, fresh tomato, and onion. In a blender cup or blender, mix the cilantro, basil, chipotle, sun-dried tomatoes, and olive oil. Blend until the consistency is that of a chunky paste. Add to the large bowl and mix well. Add the sea salt and lemon juice. Mix well. Cover and refrigerate the salsa for 1 to 4 hours, until the flavors mingle.

Tomatillo Salsa

Tomatillos have a high entertainment value because nature decided to make this fruit come complete with wrapping paper. A tomatillo is like a cross between a berry and a green tomato and has papery husk surrounding its fruit. Serve with sliced veggies (such as sunchokes, carrots, or jicama), for dipping. SERVES 4

1 pound tomatillos, husked and diced (about 3 cups)

1 cup pitted and diced olives

1/2 cup diced yellow bell pepper

1/4 cup diced tomato

1/2 cup diced onion

2 tablespoons minced fresh cilantro

2 tablespoons Bragg Liquid Aminos

Juice of 1 lime

1 habanero chile, seeded and minced

In a large bowl, mix the tomatillos, olives, bell pepper, tomato, onion, and cilantro. Add the Braggs and lime juice and mix well. Add the habanero to taste. Cover and let sit in the refrigerator or at room temperature for 1 to 4 hours, until the flavors mingle. Serve with sliced veggies for dipping.

Chile Mole

Many ingredients go into making a good mole. In Mexico, chocolate or cacao is traditionally used in its preparation. This mole features a range of vegetables and incorporates many layers of flavor. SERVES 4

1 large tomato, diced

1/2 red bell pepper, seeded and diced

1/2 purple or yellow bell pepper, seeded and diced

1 medium avocado, peeled, pitted, and cubed

1 1/2 cups corn kernels (approximately 3 ears corn)

1/4 cup loosely packed fresh flat-leaf parsley leaves

1/4 cup loosely packed fresh cilantro leaves

1/2 cup dry-packed sun-dried tomatoes, soaked in water until soft and drained

2 tablespoons Bragg Liquid Aminos

2 cloves garlic, pressed

Juice of 1/2 lemon

1 teaspoon nutritional yeast

Pinch of cayenne pepper

In a bowl, mix the tomato, bell peppers, avocado, and corn. Place the parsley, cilantro, sun-dried tomatoes, Braggs, garlic, lemon juice, and yeast in a blender and blend until creamy. Season with the cayenne. Add the blended mixture to the bowl containing the diced vegetables. Stir until all of the ingredients are evenly combined and a thick consistency is achieved.

Pea Mole

Sometimes avocados aren't available, yet we still crave a good guacamole. This pea mole is a great substitute for these occasions. Fresh peas are less oily than avocados but are just as creamy. Serve with cucumber slices or Corn Chips (page 90). SERVES 4

3 cups shelled fresh peas (approximately 3 pounds peas in their pods)

¼ cup loosely packed fresh cilantro leaves

Juice of 1 lime

Pinch of sun-dried sea salt

Place the peas, cilantro, lime juice, and sea salt in a food processor and process until smooth. Serve in a bowl.

Onion-Walnut Pâté

I first made this pâté using only foraged, wild foods such as wild onions, parsley, English walnuts, and pine nuts, which all grow in Northern California and parts of the Pacific Northwest. I even served it on dandelion greens and nasturtium leaves. SERVES 2 TO 4

1 small onion, minced

¼ cup loosely packed fresh flat-leaf parsley leaves

2 cups soaked walnuts (see page 64), drained

2 teaspoons pine nuts, soaked 2 hours in water and drained (see page 64)

1 tablespoon Bragg Liquid Aminos

2 tablespoons nutritional yeast

In a homogenizing juicer, homogenize the onion, parsley, walnuts, and pine nuts into a bowl. Add the Braggs and yeast and mix well. Serve in a bowl.

Cashew-Beet Pâté

Beets have a high sugar content and cashews are possibly the sweetest nut. Together they help give this pâté a pleasantly sweet flavor. Try serving this with cucumber slices. SERVES 4

2 cups soaked cashews (see page 64), drained

2 large beets, peeled and cut into chunks

2 large carrots

$1/4$ cup minced fresh flat-leaf parsley

$1/4$ cup minced fresh cilantro

2 stalks celery, diced

$1/2$ sweet onion, minced and rinsed

1 tablespoon nutritional yeast

2 tablespoons Bragg Liquid Aminos

Using a homogenizing juicer with the blank plate in place, or a very strong food processor, grind the cashews, beets, carrots, parsley, and cilantro. Transfer to a bowl and mix in the celery, onion, yeast, and Braggs and serve.

Sunny Red Pepper Pâté

The sunflower spends its days following the sun as it journeys across the heavens. It is fun to notice how sunflowers face east in the morning and west in the evening. This recipe features sprouted sunflower seeds. SERVES 4

2 cups sunflower sprouts (see page 20)

1/2 cup soaked almonds (see page 64), drained

1 large red bell pepper, seeded and chopped

1 clove garlic, pressed

2 tablespoons chopped fresh dill

2 tablespoons chopped fresh cilantro

1 red onion, minced and rinsed

Juice of 1 lemon

2 tablespoons Bragg Liquid Aminos

2 tablespoons nutritional yeast

In a homogenizing juicer or food processor, grind the sunflower sprouts, almonds, bell pepper, garlic, and herbs. Transfer to a bowl. Stir in the onion, lemon juice, Braggs, and yeast and serve.

Carrot-Almond Pâté

This pâté was the house standard at The Raw Experience. Many of the restaurant's dishes, such as the sampler supreme, nori rolls, and even our "rawich," included this pâté. This is a very versatile recipe; try it stuffed in a hollowed-out cucumber or alongside Corn Chips (page 90). SERVES 4

9 large carrots

2 cups almonds, sprouted for 1 day (see page 20)

1/4 cup loosely packed fresh flat-leaf parsley leaves

1/4 cup loosely packed fresh cilantro leaves

1/4 cup minced onion, rinsed

5 tablespoons Bragg Liquid Aminos

2 tablespoons nutritional yeast

1 tablespoon olive oil

Using a homogenizing juicer with the blank plate in place, homogenize the carrots, almonds, parsley, and cilantro into a bowl. Mix in the onion, Braggs, yeast, and olive oil and serve.

Unstuffing

For Thanksgiving, I love to re-create traditional dishes in untraditional ways. This unstuffing is a hit at every Thanksgiving dinner I've attended. SERVES 2 TO 4

1 large loaf or 2 small loaves
Herbed Essence Bread
(page 171), crumbled
(about 4 cups)

¼ onion, minced and rinsed

2 stalks celery minced

2 carrots, shredded

¼ cup sunflower seeds

1 teaspoon caraway seeds

2 tablespoons nutritional yeast

2 to 3 tablespoons Bragg
Liquid Aminos

In a large bowl, mix the bread crumbs, onion, celery, and carrots. In a blender cup or a spice grinder, pulverize the sunflower and caraway seeds. Add the seeds to the bowl containing the bread crumb mixture. Add the yeast and up to 3 tablespoons of the Braggs, to taste, and stir well.

Cranberry Sauce

Tart and tangy, this cranberry sauce is a welcome addition to any feast. SERVES 4

3 cups fresh cranberries, or
1½ cups dried cranberries,
soaked in water until soft
and drained

5 seeded, soaked dates
(see page 64), drained

1 cup soaked raisins
(see page 64), drained

1 teaspoon ground allspice

¼ cup freshly squeezed
orange juice

Place all of the ingredients in a blender and blend until smooth. Transfer to a bowl, cover, and refrigerate until chilled before serving.

Basic Seed Cheeze

Cultured food is one of the four living food groups, along with fresh foods, sprouted foods, and dried foods. Seed cheeze, a cultured food, is a great way to maintain healthy flora in your digestive system. This basic version, like tofu, is very versatile and can be used in many recipes that call for tofu. Seed cheeze can be made from any seed, although sunflower and pumpkin seeds seem to work the best. Dr. Ann Wigmore, the mother of sprouts and wheatgrass, taught me how to make seed cheeze during my time at her school, Dr. Ann Wigmore's Institute for Living Food Studies. This dish is one of the foundations of the living food movement. MAKES 4 CUPS

3 cups sunflower, pumpkin, or sesame seeds

Filtered water

1 tablespoon Rejuvelac (page 84) or whey starter (optional)

Place the sunflower seeds in a $\frac{1}{2}$-gallon glass jar and fill the jar to the top with the water. Cover with a cloth, screen, or mesh and soak overnight. The next morning, drain and rinse the seeds. Place the seeds in a food processor and pulse with 2 cups fresh water a few times, until chunky. Pour into a clean jar and cover with cheesecloth. If desired, add the rejuvelac or whey starter to make the seeds culture faster. Place the jar in a dark, warm place for 10 to 12 hours, or only 6 to 8 hours if rejuvelac was added.

The curds (solid part) and whey (liquid part) should separate. The seed cheeze should smell slightly sour and cultured, like yogurt. Drain off as much whey as you can, reserving it for other uses. Squeeze the curds in a piece of cheesecloth to remove the remaining whey. (If you do this over a bowl you can save this whey, too.) The dry curds are the seed cheeze and are now ready for use. To store or shape the cheeze, pack it into a bowl or container, cover, and refrigerate for up to 2 days.

Festive Seed Cheeze

This colorful version of seed cheeze played a key part in The Raw Experience's nori rolls (page 193) and earned many smiles from the residents of Maui. MAKES 5 CUPS

¼ cup pine nuts

2 cups Basic Seed Cheeze (page 166), prepared using sunflower seeds

1 small carrot, shredded

½ yellow bell pepper, diced

1 small beet, peeled and shredded

¼ cup minced onion, rinsed

¼ cup minced fresh flat-leaf parsley leaves

¼ cup minced fresh cilantro leaves

3 tablespoons Bragg Liquid Aminos

Juice of ½ lemon

Pinch of nutritional yeast

Using a blender cup or blender, grind the pine nuts into a fine powder. In a large bowl, combine the ground pine nuts, seed cheeze, carrot, bell pepper, beet, and onion. Add the parsley, cilantro, Braggs, lemon juice, and yeast, and mix well. Serve.

Pumpkin-Cashew Seed Cheeze

This recipe includes pumpkin and cheeze. Pumpkin seeds are rich and oily and add a heartier flavor to this dish. To make pumpkin seed cheeze, just follow the instructions for Basic Seed Cheeze, using pumpkin seeds. MAKES 3½ CUPS

2 cups Basic Seed Cheeze (page 166), prepared using sunflower seeds

1 cup soaked cashews (see page 64), drained

½ cup Basic Seed Cheeze (page 166), prepared using pumpkin seeds

3 tablespoons Bragg Liquid Aminos

In a food processor, blend all of the ingredients together until smooth. Transfer to a large bowl and serve.

Rich and Creamy Seed Cheeze

Avocado trees can grow almost anywhere, although they'll usually only bear fruit in the tropics. In New York City, my mother has grown an avocado tree for more than twenty-five years. It is kept inside because avocados don't enjoy the cold. It may never fruit, but it's nice to know it is there. MAKES 3 CUPS

1 avocado, peeled and pitted

2 cups Basic Seed Cheeze (page 166), prepared using sunflower seeds

¼ cup minced fresh flat-leaf parsley

1 teaspoon nutritional yeast

2 tablespoons Bragg Liquid Aminos

In a large bowl, mash the avocado. Stir in the seed cheeze, parsley, yeast, and Braggs. Serve.

Herbed Garlic Seed Cheeze

With its garlic and basil, this cheeze has an Italian flair. SERVES 4

5 dry-packed sun-dried tomatoes

2 cups Basic Seed Cheeze (page 166), prepared using equal amounts of sunflower and sesame seeds

2 tablespoons chopped fresh basil

2 tablespoons chopped fresh flat-leaf parsley

2 tablespoons chopped fresh cilantro

2 cloves garlic, crushed

2 tablespoons Bragg Liquid Aminos

In a small bowl, soak the tomatoes in water to cover until soft. Drain and mince. In a large bowl, combine the tomatoes, seed cheeze, herbs, garlic and Braggs. Mix well and serve with a smile.

Colorful Tofu Salad

Eye appeal is important in any dish you create. Sometimes eye appeal is about symmetry and use of complementary colors. In this dish, the vegetables create a medley of hues in contrast to the white tofu background; it is bright and stunning to look at. SERVES 4

2 cups Basic Tofu (page 93)

1 small carrot, shredded

2 small beets, peeled and shredded

½ small onion, diced

½ red bell pepper, seeded and diced

1 tablespoon Bragg Liquid Aminos

1 teaspoon ground cumin

In a large bowl, combine the tofu, carrot, beets, onion, and bell pepper. Stir in the Braggs and cumin and serve.

Tapenade

Olives and sun-dried tomatoes are two of the richest and most concentrated flavors that raw food offers. Combining the two yields this classic Italian spread. Serve with Herbed Essence Bread (page 171) or zucchini slices. SERVES 2 TO 4

8 dry-packed sun-dried tomatoes, soaked in water until soft and drained

15 pitted olives

2 tablespoons Bragg Liquid Aminos

1 clove garlic

3 sprigs basil

Herbed Essence Bread (page 171) or zucchini slices, for serving

Grind all of the ingredients in a food processor until smooth. Transfer to a bowl and serve.

Essence Breads

This bread was originally called "Essene Bread." The Essenes were a group of people living thousands of years ago in Palestine. The tradition of making Essene bread is discussed in the Essene Gospels, a translation of the Dead Sea Scrolls. The Essenes would sprout their grains, mash them up, and set them in the sun to dry. This sacred bread-making tradition has been handed down over the ages. I decided to change the name to Essence Bread because the loaves hold the essence of life. Sprouted grains have a great amount of potential energy, and drying them in the sun concentrates the essential life force contained within.

Essence Breads are created by sprouting grains such as wheat, rye, oat, and kamut or seeds like buckwheat. These grains and seeds are then dried at a low enough temperature (108°F) to ensure enzyme protection. Essence Breads can be used as a live alternative to overly processed baked bread, in rawiches or as pizza crusts. You can dry Essence Breads slightly for a soft, doughy texture, or dry the bread totally for a crispy texture that makes great chips and crackers and increases its storage time.

Grains are at their nutritional peak when the sprouting tail is as long as the grain itself. I recommend processing the sprouted grains through a homogenizing juicer with the juicing plate and adding a small amount of water to keep it lubricated. (Added water is needed only when the grains aren't already moist and even—then, just 1 or 2 tablespoons per cup of grains will do the job.) Be sure to put a container where the juice normally comes out to catch excess gluten or water. Too much gluten can be difficult to pass through the body. Removing the glutinous part of the grain makes for easier digestion, especially of wheat, a grain known for its high gluten content. Buckwheat contains no gluten and makes awesome bread. The pulp that comes out of the front of the juicer is the usable part of the grain. If a homogenizing juicer is unavailable, the grain can be ground in a food processor, adding just enough water to form a smooth paste. The dough can be shaped into loaves, sticks, or flat crusts.

Herbed Essence Bread

Breads made with herbs are aromatic and savory. In addition to traditional square loaves, this bread may be pressed into flat circles or squares, rounded loaves, or even stars or hearts. MAKES 4 LOAVES

2 cups sprouted grain (see page 20), such as wheat, rye, kamut, quinoa, or barley

2 tablespoons minced fresh flat-leaf parsley

2 tablespoons minced fresh cilantro

2 tablespoons minced fresh basil

1/4 cup shredded carrot

2 tablespoons minced onion

1 clove garlic, pressed

2 cups flax seeds

Grind the grain in a homogenizing juicer and place it in a large bowl. Add the parsley, cilantro, basil, carrot, onion, and garlic to the grain and mix well. In a blender cup or blender, grind the flax seeds into a fine powder. Add the flax powder to the bowl and mix well. Divide the dough into 4 equal portions and press each into a loaf or another shape. Using one of the methods described on page 28, dehydrate the bread for 8 hours and flip. Dry for 12 to 15 hours more, depending on the moisture level desired.

Apple-Cinnamon Essence Bread

This bread is a great breakfast treat. It tastes like apple turnovers. MAKES 4 LOAVES

4 cups sprouted grain (see page 20), such as wheat, buckwheat, or kamut

7 seeded, soaked dates (see page 64), drained

1 cup shredded apples (1 to 2 apples)

1 cup chopped walnuts

2 teaspoons ground cinnamon

Grind the grain, dates, and apples in a homogenizing juicer and place in a large bowl. Stir in the walnuts and cinnamon and mix thoroughly. Divide the dough into 4 equal portions and press each into a loaf or another shape. Using one of the methods described on page 28, dehydrate the bread for 8 hours and flip. Dry for 12 to 15 hours more, depending on the moisture level desired.

Carrot-Almond Essence Bread

Carrot bread is very much like a doughy carrot cake. This bread is a great breakfast treat. MAKES 4 LOAVES

4 cups sprouted grain (see page 20), such as rye or wheat

5 seeded, soaked dates (see page 64), drained

1 cup sprouted almonds (see page 20)

2 carrots, shredded (about 2 cups)

2 teaspoons soaked caraway seeds (see page 64), drained

Grind the grain in a homogenizing juicer and place in a large bowl. In a blender cup or blender, pulse the dates and the almonds until they form a thick paste. Add the date mixture to the bowl containing the grain. Add the carrots and caraway seeds and mix thoroughly. Divide the dough into 4 equal portions and press each into a loaf or another shape. Using one of the methods described on page 28, dehydrate the bread for 8 hours and flip. Dry for 12 to 15 hours more, depending on the moisture level desired.

Fruit and Nut Essence Bread

Sweet breads are especially good for almond butter and jelly rawiches or as a simple, delicious snack, all on their own. MAKES 4 LOAVES

4 cups sprouted grain (see page 20), such as kamut or rye

5 seeded, soaked dates (see page 64), drained

1/4 cup sprouted almonds (see page 20)

1/4 cup soaked raisins (see page 64), drained

2 tablespoons chopped walnuts

Grind the grain in a homogenizing juicer and place in a large bowl. In a blender cup or blender, pulse the dates and almonds until chunky. Add the date mixture to the bowl containing the grain. Add the raisins and the walnuts and mix thoroughly. Divide the mixture into 4 equal portions and press each into a loaf or half-dome shape, 2 to 3 inches at peak. Using one of the methods described on page 28, dehydrate the bread for 8 hours and flip. Dry for 12 to 15 hours more, depending on the moisture level desired.

Caraway-Onion Essence Bread

This savory bread has a nice spicy taste to it. MAKES 4 LOAVES

2 cups sprouted grain (see page 20), such as buckwheat or rye

1 small onion, diced

1 clove garlic

¼ cup soaked caraway seeds (see page 64), drained

Grind all of the ingredients in a homogenizing juicer, place in a large bowl, and mix thoroughly. Divide the dough into 4 equal portions and press each into a loaf or another shape. Using one of the methods described on page 28, dehydrate the bread for 8 hours and flip. Dry for 12 to 15 hours more, depending on the moisture level desired.

Pumpkin Butter

Pumpkins are a cucurbit and, like most of their cousins, have a slightly starchy and bitter taste when eaten raw. Soaking pumpkins can greatly improve their flavor. Serve this spread on Fruit and Nut Essence Bread (page 172) or topped with Nut Crème (page 198) as a dessert. SERVES 4

1 pumpkin (approximately 3 pounds), such as sugar pie pumpkin or sweet pumpkin

Juice of 1 lemon

1 cup soaked pecans (see page 64), drained

1 cup seeded, soaked dates (see page 64), drained

1 teaspoon ground cinnamon

1 teaspoon freshly ground nutmeg

1 teaspoon pure vanilla extract

Peel and seed the pumpkin, reserving the seeds for another use. Cut the flesh into chunks (you should have about 4 cups). Place the pumpkin flesh in a large bowl, cover with water, add the lemon juice, and soak overnight. Drain and rinse the pumpkin and drain again.

In a homogenizing juicer, homogenize the pumpkin with the pecans and dates and place in a large bowl. Mix in the cinnamon, nutmeg, and vanilla and serve.

Baba Ghanoush

This Middle Eastern dish is hearty and earthy. The longer you marinate the eggplant, the better it gets. Serve the baba ghanoush with Sprouted Hummus (below), Falafel (page 182), or Tabouli (page 144). SERVES 4

1 large eggplant, seeded and thinly sliced

Generous pinch of sun-dried sea salt

Juice of 1 lemon

1 clove garlic, crushed

1 teaspoon sprouted cumin seeds (see page 20)

¼ cup raw tahini

1 onion, minced and rinsed

¼ cup minced fresh flat-leaf parsley

Bragg Liquid Aminos

Put the eggplant in a large bowl, cover with water, add the sea salt and lemon juice, and soak for 4 to 10 hours. (This will help cure the eggplant and improve its flavor.) Drain.

In a homogenizing juicer with the blank plate in place, homogenize the eggplant with the garlic and cumin sprouts into a large bowl. Add the tahini, onion, and parsley and mix well. Stir in the Braggs to taste and serve.

Sprouted Hummus

Garbanzo beans, also known as chickpeas, sprout easily and quickly. When sprouting garbanzos, make certain not to overfill the jar. Garbanzos expand so rapidly that they can shatter a glass jar. The best flavor comes from using garbanzos that have been sprouted for one day. SERVES 4

4 cups sprouted garbanzo beans (see page 20)

¼ cup chopped fresh flat-leaf parsley

1 clove garlic

¼ cup raw tahini

¼ cup freshly squeezed lemon juice

Sun-dried sea salt

In a homogenizing juicer with the blank plate in place, homogenize the garbanzo beans, parsley, and garlic into a bowl. Place the tahini and lemon juice in a blender and blend. Stir the lemon-tahini mixture into the bean mixture. Add sea salt to taste and serve.

Entrees

Tribal Wild Rice Salad 177

Mexican Wild Rice and Tofu 178

Festive Sprouted Wild Rice 179

Tamales 179

Tofu Loaf 180

Almond-Corn Croquettes 181

Sunflower-Carrot Croquettes 181

Falafel 182

Middle Eastern Plate 182

Angel Hair with Marinara 184

Lasagna 185

Pesto Pizza and Traditional Pizza 186

Focaccia 188

Thai Curry 191

Nori Rolls 193

Shangri La 194

Tribal Wild Rice Salad

Wild rice grows as a seed along the banks of the Great Lakes. Native Americans known as the Chippewa still hand-harvest the wild rice in the traditional manner of their tribe: one person steers the canoe while the other pulls the plants into the boat, threshing the rice from its shaft. Wild rice is one of the few seeds that will sprout anaerobically (without oxygen). Soak the wild rice for 3 to 5 days, changing the water twice a day. Look for hulled hemp seeds in health food stores. SERVES 4 TO 6

DRESSING

4 seeded, soaked dates (see page 64), drained

3 to 5 tablespoons Bragg Liquid Aminos or nama shoyu

Juice of 1 lemon

1 teaspoon flax oil

2 cups sprouted wild rice (see page 20)

1 avocado, peeled, pitted, and cubed

1 yellow bell pepper, seeded and diced

1 Maui or other sweet onion, minced and rinsed

1 Roma tomato, diced

1 mango, peeled, pitted, and diced

¼ cup hulled hemp seeds

Black and white sesame seeds, for garnish

Chopped almonds, for garnish

Yellow bell pepper strips, for garnish

To prepare the dressing, place the dates, 3 tablespoons of the Braggs, the lemon juice, and flax oil in a blender and process until creamy. Add up to 2 tablespoons of the remaining Braggs to taste.

In a large bowl, combine the sprouted rice, avocado, bell pepper, onion, tomato, mango, and hemp seeds. Add the dressing and toss well.

To prepare each serving, line a 2-cup bowl with plastic wrap and fill with salad, packing the salad firmly as you go until level. Place an individual serving plate over the top of the bowl and invert. Set the bowl aside and slowly peel away the plastic wrap. Repeat for the remaining servings. Top each with a sprinkling of sesame seeds and almonds. Garnish the edges of the plate with the bell pepper strips and serve.

Mexican Wild Rice and Tofu

In many places, rice is a staple, or primary food source. Wild rice is very adaptable and can be seasoned with a variety of ingredients. This entrée has a decidedly Mexican flair. SERVES 4

3 cups sprouted wild rice (see page 20)

2 small tomatoes, diced

2 tablespoons diced onion

2 tablespoons minced fresh cilantro

1 red bell pepper, seeded and diced

1 yellow bell pepper, seeded and diced

1 clove garlic, pressed

$1/4$ cup Bragg Liquid Aminos, or 1 teaspoon sun-dried sea salt

$1/2$ teaspoon chile powder

$1/2$ teaspoon cayenne pepper

Juice of $1/2$ lime

2 cups Basic Tofu (page 93) or Basic Seed Cheeze (page 166)

In a large bowl, combine the rice, tomatoes, onion, cilantro, bell peppers, and garlic. Add the Braggs, chile powder, cayenne pepper, and lime juice, and toss well. Serve with the tofu or seed cheeze.

Festive Sprouted Wild Rice

Sprouted black long-grain wild rice has a robust taste and smell. The seeds sprout in water, which you change twice a day. When the seeds are rinsed, the earthy aroma rises up. Take a deep inhalation as you pour out the water, and enjoy the scent.

SERVES 4 TO 6

5 cups sprouted wild rice
(see page 20)

1/2 onion, minced and rinsed

1 red bell pepper, seeded
and diced

1 cup corn kernels
(approximately 2 ears corn)

5 tablespoons Bragg
Liquid Aminos

3 tablespoons paprika

Juice of 1 orange

In a large bowl, combine the rice, onion, bell pepper, and corn. Stir in the Braggs, paprika, and orange juice and serve.

Tamales

This raw adaptation of the classic Mexican dish is simple to make and tastes delicious.

SERVES 4

1 cup flax seeds

6 cups corn kernels
(approximately 12 ears corn)

1 cup dried cilantro

2 teaspoons sun-dried sea salt

2 cups Mexican Wild Rice
and Tofu (page 178)

1 cup Red Pepper–Chipotle Salsa
(page 158)

1 cup Star Fruit Guacamole
(page 156)

In a coffee grinder or food processor, grind the flax seeds into a fine powder. In a food processor, blend the corn, cilantro, salt, and flax powder until well combined but still chunky. Form into 4 patties, each 1/2 inch thick and 6 inches in diameter, arrange on dehydrator sheets or a piece of waxed paper on a flat tray, and dry for 8 to 10 hours (see page 28). Top each patty with 1/2 cup of the rice, 1/4 cup of the salsa, and 1/4 cup of the guacamole. Enjoy!

Tofu Loaf

The sprouted tofu gives this dish a nice light texture while still having a very meaty taste. For a richer version, use seed cheeze (see pages 166 to 168) in place of the tofu.
SERVES 4

2 cups Basic Tofu (page 93)

1 cup carrot pulp (from juicing carrots)

1/2 onion, chopped

1/2 stalk celery, chopped

2 cloves garlic, minced

1/4 cup minced fresh flat-leaf parsley

1/4 cup raw tahini

2 tablespoons Bragg Liquid Aminos

1 tablespoon nutritional yeast

In a large bowl, combine all of the ingredients and mix thoroughly. Line a loaf pan with a piece of plastic wrap and press the tofu mixture firmly into the pan. Invert the loaf pan onto a plate. Gently remove the loaf pan and set aside, then carefully peel away the plastic wrap. Alternatively, you can use your hands to form the tofu mixture into a loaf shape. Serve.

Almond-Corn Croquettes

We served this evolution of croquettes at The Raw Experience during a Living Thanksgiving celebration on Maui. SERVES 4

1 cup sunflower seeds

1 cup flax seeds

2 cups sprouted almonds
(see page 20)

4 cups corn kernels
(approximately 8 ears corn)

2 tablespoons Bragg
Liquid Aminos

1/4 cup diced onion

Almond-Cumin Dressing
(page 146), for drizzling

2 loaves Caraway-Onion Essence
Bread (page 173), for serving

In a coffee grinder or food processor, grind the sunflower and flax seeds into a fine powder. In a homogenizing juicer or a food processor, homogenize or finely grind the seed powders, sprouted almonds, corn, Braggs, and onion and place in a large bowl. Form the mixture into small, 1½-inch loaves. Arrange on a serving plate, drizzle with the salad dressing, and serve, accompanied by the bread.

Sunflower-Carrot Croquettes

I first created this delightful little dish for a housewarming party that I was having. I served the croquettes shaped into stars and hearts, and people loved them. SERVES 4

6 carrots, chopped

3 cups soaked sunflower seeds
(see page 64), drained

1 cup chopped fresh cilantro

1/4 cup diced onion

3 tablespoons Bragg Liquid
Aminos

2 tablespoons nutritional yeast

Fresh herbs (such as flat-leaf
parsley or dill), for garnish

In a homogenizing juicer, homogenize the carrots and sunflower seeds into a large bowl. Mix in the cilantro, onion, Braggs, and yeast and form into shapes such as circles, stars, or hearts. Arrange on a serving platter, garnish with fresh herbs, and serve.

Falafel

These falafels can be prepared as crusts for use in the Middle Eastern Plate (see below), or they can be made into more traditional falafel balls. To make the balls, just follow the instructions below but roll the mixture into 1-inch balls, then dehydrate them for only 8 to 10 hours. (Pictured opposite) MAKES FOUR 8-INCH CRUSTS OR EIGHT 4-INCH CRUSTS

6 cups sprouted garbanzo beans (see page 20)

1 cup loosely packed fresh flat-leaf parsley leaves

1 cup raw tahini

1 cup freshly squeezed lemon juice

1 onion, minced

2 tablespoons ground cumin

6 tablespoons Bragg Liquid Aminos, or 2 tablespoons sun-dried sea salt

1 cup sesame seeds

Using a homogenizing juicer with the blank plate in place, homogenize the garbanzo beans and parsley and place in a large bowl. Place the tahini, lemon juice, onion, cumin, and Braggs in a blender and blend. Stir the tahini mixture into the garbanzo paste. In a spice grinder, grind the sesame seeds into a fine powder. Mix into the garbanzo paste. Press into $1/4$-inch-thick crusts, each 4 or 8 inches in diameter. Using one of the methods described on page 28, dehydrate for 12 to 14 hours, flipping at least once during the drying time.

Middle Eastern Plate

This recipe uses garbanzo beans to make both the falafel-style pizza crust and the hummus spread. SERVES 4

4 falafel crusts (page 182)

2 cups Sprouted Hummus (page 174)

1 tomato, diced

$1/4$ cup minced onion, rinsed

2 tablespoons diced cucumber

2 tablespoons minced fresh curly parsley

4 sprigs mint, for garnish

4 black olives, for garnish

Place each of the falafel crusts on an individual serving plate. Spread $1/2$ cup of the hummus on top of each crust. Sprinkle the tomato, onion, cucumber, and parsley evenly over the top of each crust. Garnish with the mint and olives and serve.

Angel Hair with Marinara

I have always been a strong believer that the key to pasta is in the sauce, not in the pasta. Spaghetti is just flour and water, much like papier-mâché. The noodles are just a carrier. Serve with a green salad and Italian Dressing (page 152) and Herbed Essence Bread (page 171) cut into triangles. SERVES 4

2 large zucchini

1 large yellow summer squash

1 large, fat carrot

1 large red beet

Pinch of sun-dried sea salt

2 cups Red Sauce (page 95)

1/2 cup pine nuts, finely ground

1/2 cup pitted and sliced olives

1/8 cup chopped fresh basil

5 dry-packed sun-dried tomatoes, soaked in water until soft, drained, and finely chopped

Herbed Essence Bread (page 171), cut into triangles, for serving

Use a spiralizer to create spaghetti-like strands or a vegetable peeler to create linguini-shaped "pasta" using the zucchini, squash, carrot, and beet. Rinse the vegetables well and soak in water with the salt for 1 hour. Drain.

In each of 4 serving bowls, place one-quarter of the vegetables. Pour 1/2 cup of the red sauce over each serving. Top each serving with some of the pine nuts, olives, basil, and sun-dried tomatoes and serve with the bread.

Lasagna

One of the claims to fame of The Raw Experience was that we could make any cooked-food dish in a raw way. We got a number of requests for a raw lasagna and created this recipe in response. For a while we called it "Living," but eventually we went back to its original name. Versions of this dish are served in raw food and vegetarian restaurants throughout America. SERVES 4 TO 8

1 cup filtered water

1 cup freshly squeezed lemon juice

3 tablespoons Bragg Liquid Aminos

1 clove garlic, pressed

1 teaspoon dried parsley

1 teaspoon dried basil

1 eggplant, peeled

2 large zucchini, peeled

1 sweet onion, cut into rings

1 cup chopped walnuts

4 cups Red Sauce (page 95)

2 cups White Sauce (page 95)

In a bowl, combine the water, lemon juice, Braggs, garlic, parsley, and basil. Using a vegetable peeler or mandoline with the thinnest blade, slice the eggplant and zucchini lengthwise into long strips. Place the eggplant, zucchini, and onion in a shallow dish and pour the lemon juice mixture over the top. Marinate overnight.

In a blender cup or coffee grinder, grind the walnuts into a fine powder. Moisten the inside of a lasagna dish with water and sprinkle the bottom and sides of the dish with 2 tablespoons of the walnut powder to coat. Cover the bottom of the dish with a layer of the marinated vegetables and top with 1 cup of the red sauce and $^1/_2$ cup of the white sauce. Repeat three more times. Top with the remaining walnut powder and serve, or dehydrate for 4 hours to concentrate the flavors and then serve.

Pesto Pizza and Traditional Pizza

At The Raw Experience in San Francisco, we always came up with different pizzas as a daily special, but these two were permanently on the menu. SERVES 4

4 (8-inch) Pizza Crusts (recipe follows)

1 cup Red Sauce (page 95)

1 cup White Sauce (page 95)

1 cup Presto Pesto (page 89)

$1/2$ red tomato, diced

$1/2$ yellow tomato, diced

1 onion, minced and rinsed

1 small beet, peeled and shredded

$1/2$ cup pine nuts, ground

5 purple basil leaves, minced

5 green basil leaves, minced

Place each of the crusts on an individual serving plate. Spread $1/2$ cup of the red sauce over each of two of the crusts, followed by $1/2$ cup of the white sauce over each. Spread $1/2$ cup of the pesto on each of the two remaining crusts. Top all four with the tomatoes, onion, beet, pine nuts, and basil and serve.

PIZZA CRUSTS

MAKES FOUR 8-INCH CRUSTS OR EIGHT 4-INCH CRUSTS

4 cups sprouted wheat (see page 20)

1 clove garlic, pressed

$^1/_4$ cup minced fresh flat-leaf parsley

$^1/_4$ cup minced fresh cilantro

$^1/_4$ cup minced fresh basil

$^1/_4$ cup sprouted cumin seeds (see page 20)

$^1/_4$ cup soaked flax seeds (see page 64), drained

1 beet, peeled and shredded

2 carrots, shredded

$^1/_2$ cup minced onion

3 tablespoons Bragg Liquid Aminos

Using a homogenizing juicer, homogenize the wheat sprouts with the garlic, parsley, cilantro, basil, and cumin and flax seeds. Place in a large bowl and mix in the beet, carrot, onion, and Braggs. Stir until well mixed, and then press into $^1/_4$-inch-thick crusts, each 4 or 8 inches in diameter. Using one of the methods described on page 28, dehydrate the crusts for 12 hours, flipping at least once during the drying time.

Focaccia

This vegetable-topped bread is a classic Italian meal. It's like pizza without the sauces. SERVES 4

GARLIC-HERB OIL

¹/₂ cup olive or flax oil

1 or 2 cloves garlic, pressed

4 leaves fresh basil

1 teaspoon minced fresh rosemary

2 cups dry-packed sun-dried tomatoes, soaked in water until soft, drained, and finely chopped

2 red bell peppers, seeded and diced

10 pitted olives, sliced crosswise

1 small sweet onion, minced

1 cup pine nuts, finely ground

¹/₂ cup chopped fresh basil

4 (8-inch) Pizza Crusts (page 187) or Herbed Essence Breads (page 171)

To prepare the Garlic-Herb Oil, in a bowl, combine all of the ingredients. Cover and allow to sit overnight.

In a bowl, combine the sun-dried tomatoes, bell peppers, olives, onion, pine nuts, and basil. Place each of the crusts on an individual serving plate. Spread ¹/₄ cup to ¹/₂ cup of the sun-dried tomato mixture over each crust. Drizzle each focaccia with the Garlic-Herb Oil and serve.

Thai Curry

Thailand has been heavily influenced by Indian culture. India's religion, music, and especially their food have all become part of Thailand's heritage. Curries are often thought of as an Indian thing, but Thai versions of curry are just as divine. Serve this dish with Tom Yum (page 120), if desired. SERVES 4

CURRY SAUCE

1½-inch piece fresh ginger

1 cup soaked peanuts (see page 64), drained

1 cup fresh, finely chopped young coconut meat (see page 50)

½ cup coconut water

1 tablespoon raw almond butter

2 teaspoons Bragg Liquid Aminos

1 clove garlic, pressed

1 teaspoon turmeric

1 teaspoon curry powder

Juice of 1 orange

1 Thai chile

¼ head cauliflower, diced

1 small carrot, shredded

¼ head red cabbage, shredded

½ large cucumber, peeled and cut into half-moons

Basil leaves, for garnish

Mung bean sprouts, for garnish

To prepare the sauce, finely grate the ginger on a ginger grater or fine grater to extract the juice (you should have about 1 tablespoon). Place the ginger juice, peanuts, coconut meat, coconut water, almond butter, Braggs, garlic, turmeric, curry powder, and orange juice in a blender and blend until smooth. Add the Thai chile to taste.

Place the cauliflower, carrot, cabbage, and cucumber in a bowl. Pour the sauce over the vegetables, garnish with the basil and bean sprouts, and serve.

Nori Rolls

This was the most popular dish ever at The Raw Experience, where we would some-times make up to fifty nori rolls a day. Nori can be rolled using a bamboo sushi mat or by hand. Once it is rolled, it takes skill to cut. Be sure to use a wet serrated knife and to keep the seam side down. It takes skill and patience to master nori rolling and cutting, but once you figure it out, it's a snap. Nori is very versatile, and many different things can be rolled inside. Experiment with your own favorite flavors.

SERVES 4

4 sheets nori (dried, not toasted)

3 cups loosely packed field greens

1 cup Festive Seed Cheeze (page 167)

1 cup Carrot-Almond Pâté (page 164)

1 avocado, peeled, pitted, and sliced

1 carrot, cut into $1/8$-inch-thick strips

1 beet, peeled and cut into $1/8$-inch-thick strips

1 cup loosely packed sunflower sprouts (see page 20)

$1/4$ cup sesame seeds, for garnish

For each roll, place a nori sheet on a sushi mat or the counter, shiny side down with the ridges running vertically. Lay a few greens on the sheet 1 inch from one edge. Cover with $1/4$ cup of the seed cheeze and $1/4$ cup of the pâté. Top with one-quarter each of the avocado, carrot, beet, and sprouts. Fold the nori sheet in half and firmly envelop the contents by tucking the folded sheet edge underneath the contents. Roll the nori sheet into a cylinder, wrapping the contents firmly. Moisten the outside edge of the nori sheet and seal. Let sit, seam side down, for 2 minutes. Cut into 8 to 10 serving pieces with a wet serrated knife. Serve garnished with the sesame seeds.

Shangri La

The mystic land of the immortals is known in the Far East as Shangri La, and this dish will transport you there. This Asian-inspired dish is a delicious remedy for a stir-fry craving. When it was first invented, it was actually called "Stir-Free." SERVES 4

¼ cup Bragg Liquid Aminos

1½ cups filtered water

Juice of 1 lemon

1 head broccoli, chopped

1 large carrot, shredded

½ small head napa cabbage, shredded

SEVEN-STAR SAUCE

3-inch piece fresh ginger

1 cup pine nuts, soaked 2 hours and drained

4 seeded, soaked dates (see page 64), drained

2 tablespoons raw tahini

2 tablespoons white miso

Filtered water as needed

¼ cup chopped green onion, for garnish

1 tablespoon black sesame seeds, for garnish

In a large bowl, combine the Braggs, water, and lemon juice. Add the broccoli, carrot, and cabbage. Let sit for 1 hour or up to 10 hours.

To prepare the sauce, finely grate the ginger on a ginger grater or fine grater to extract its juice (you should have about 2 tablespoons). Place the ginger juice, pine nuts, dates, tahini, and miso in a blender and blend, adding water as needed to create a creamy consistency.

Drain the marinated vegetables and transfer to a serving bowl. Pour the sauce over the vegetables and mix well. Garnish with the green onion and sesame seeds and serve.

Desserts

Carob Devastation	196
Brownies	197
Raw Fruit Pies	198
Coconut Custard	199
Lemon Bars	200
Frozen Fudge	200
Banana Bread	201
Oat-Date Rawies	201
Sesame Rawies	202
Carob-Hazelnut Torte	202
Bliss Balls	204
Cashew Sauce	204
Buckies	205
Ultimate Sundae	205
Carrot Kake	206
Six-Layer Carob Kake	207
Apple Kake	208

Carob Devastation

The creation of this recipe was a celebratory moment in the world of raw cuisine. I always told stories about a cake I loved called "chocolate devastation," which was served at an upscale restaurant named Luma, in New York City. At The Raw Experience, we came up with this raw version of a carob cake. I dubbed it Carob Devastation in honor of my favorite cake, and it became a permanent feature on our menu. SERVES 8 TO 10

1 cup sprouted almonds (see page 20)

2 cups seeded, soaked dates (see page 64), drained

1 cup soaked raisins (see page 64), drained

1 tablespoon pure vanilla extract

3 cups carrot pulp (from juicing carrots)

2 cups chopped walnuts

2 cups sunflower seeds

1 cup fresh, finely chopped coconut meat (see page 50)

1 cup raw carob powder

2 cups Nut Crème (page 198)

In a food processor, grind the almonds, dates, raisins, and vanilla. In a large bowl, mix the carrot pulp with the almond mixture. In a food processor, grind the walnuts and sunflower seeds into a fine powder. In a separate bowl, mix the powdered walnuts and sunflower seeds, the coconut, and carob. Gradually add the dry coconut mixture to the wet almond carrot mixture and stir well. On a serving plate, form into a cake shape and spread the nut crème over the top.

Brownies

These brownies were one of the first raw desserts I attempted, thanks to my friend Sena, who taught me how to make them. Whenever I visited her house, she would have these in the refrigerator waiting for me. SERVES 8 TO 10

2 cups dried figs, soaked in water until soft and drained (see page 64)

2 cups seeded, soaked dates (see page 64), drained

2 cups sprouted almonds (see page 20)

1/2 cup raw carob powder

2 tablespoons pure vanilla extract

2 cups Nut Crème (page 198)

In a homogenizing juicer with the blank plate in place, homogenize the figs, dates, and almonds into a bowl. Add the carob powder and the vanilla and mix well. Form 1/4 cup of the mixture into a 1-inch square and drizzle 2 tablespoons of the nut crème on top. Repeat for the remaining brownies. Refrigerate overnight before serving.

Raw Fruit Pies

No one is really certain who made the first raw fruit pie. I learned from Lenny Watson, Lenny learned from Viktoras Kulvinskas, and who knows where Viktoras found out about it—I haven't asked him yet. All I know is that it just keeps getting better. Our pies at The Raw Experience were "to live for," and many knew us as the folks who put the pie in Paia. These pie recipes below are really just guides. Be creative and your talent will amaze you. SERVES 8 (MAKES ONE 9-INCH PIE)

CAROB ALMOND CRUST

1 cup sprouted almonds (see page 20)

5 seeded, soaked dates (see page 64), drained

1/4 teaspoon ground cinnamon

1/4 teaspoon ground allspice

1 tablespoon raw carob powder

WALNUT ZING CRUST

1 cup sprouted walnuts (see page 20)

5 seeded, soaked dates (see page 64), drained

1/4 teaspoon ground cinnamon

1/4 teaspoon freshly grated lemon zest

PRALINE CRUST

1 cup sprouted pecans (see page 20)

5 seeded, soaked dates (see page 64), drained

1/4 teaspoon pure vanilla extract

1/4 teaspoon freshly ground nutmeg

NUT-FREE CRUST

1 cup dried banana pieces

5 seeded, soaked dates (see page 64), drained

1/4 teaspoon ground cinnamon

1/4 teaspoon ground allspice

Oil, for greasing pan (optional)

Raw carob powder, for dusting

NUT CRÈME

5 dates, seeded

1 cup filtered water

1 cup soaked nuts (such as cashews, almonds, or hazelnuts; see page 64), drained

4 cups fresh fruit pieces (such as blueberries, papaya, banana, cherimoya, sapote, or shredded coconut)

1/2 cup berries, for garnish

1 papaya, peeled, seeded, and sliced, for garnish

To prepare any of the four crusts, place all of the ingredients in a food processor and pulse a few times to combine. Continue grinding until the mixture forms a thick paste. Oil or moisten with water a 9-inch pie plate and sprinkle with the carob powder to coat (the carob powder keeps the pie crust from sticking to the plate). Form the crust mixture into a ball and press it from the center of the pie plate out toward the edges, spreading as evenly as possible. Set aside.

To prepare the nut crème, place the dates in a small bowl, cover with the water, and soak for about 1 hour, or until soft. Drain, reserving ¼ cup of the liquid. Place the dates, reserved liquid, and nuts in a blender or blender cup, and grind until smooth.

To prepare the fruit, you may slice it, purée it, leave it whole, or any combination of the three. Fill the pie crust with the prepared fruit. Top with the nut crème and garnish with the berries and papaya slices, arranged in a sunburst formation.

Coconut Custard

This smooth and creamy dessert is a Hawaiian specialty. In old Hawaii, it was a custom to plant five coconut trees for each child born. This was to provide all of the basic food, clothing, and shelter they would need. Today there is an abundance of coconuts in Hawaii, and this custard is a true "local kine" recipe. SERVES 2 TO 4

2 dates, seeded

½ cup filtered water

2 cups fresh, finely chopped young coconut meat (see page 50)

1 teaspoon pure vanilla extract

Place the dates in a small bowl, cover with the water, and soak for about 1 hour, or until soft. In a blender cup or small food processor, blend the dates along with their soaking water, the coconut, and the vanilla into a smooth custard. Spoon into individual bowls, refrigerate until chilled, and serve.

Lemon Bars

These easy snack bars dry quickly and have a tangy, sweet flavor. SERVES 4

1 cup sprouted oats (see page 20)

1 cup soaked almonds (see page 64), drained

1/2 cup seeded, soaked dates (see page 64), drained

3 tablespoons freshly grated lemon zest

Juice of 1 lemon

Using a homogenizing juicer, homogenize the oats, almonds, and dates until smooth. Transfer the mixture to a large bowl and mix in the lemon zest and juice. Press evenly into an 18-inch dehydrator tray, spreading it 1/2 inch thick. Using one of the methods described on page 28, dehydrate the bars for 18 hours. Cut out of the tray into bars and dry longer. The bars shouldn't be super sticky. Refrigerate until chilled and serve.

Frozen Fudge

This fudge is sweet and semiaddictive. Many of my students have this recipe and make it a daily staple in their homes. This stuff tastes so good and melts in your mouth—just be careful not to eat too much! SERVES 6 TO 10

1 cup dates, seeded

1 1/2 cups filtered water

1 tablespoon pure vanilla extract

1 1/2 cups nut butter (such as almond or hazelnut)

1 1/2 cups raw carob powder

1/2 cup dried shredded coconut

Place the dates in a bowl, cover with the water, and soak for about an hour, or until soft. Drain, reserving the liquid. Place the dates and vanilla in a blender and blend until smooth, slowly adding the soaking water as needed to form a creamy consistency. Transfer the date mixture to a large bowl, add the nut butter, and stir to combine. In a separate bowl, mix the carob and coconut. Gradually add the dry carob mixture to the wet date mixture. Stir well. Press evenly into a 10 by 18-inch brownie pan, 1 inch thick, and freeze until firm, about 3 hours. To serve, cut into 1-inch squares.

Banana Bread

Bananas are actually an herb plant, not a fruit, and we eat its flowering stalk. There are hundreds of varieties of bananas, and they grow wild all over Maui. A banana tree can grow from seed to fruit in just nine months. These prolific trees provide an excellent source of nourishment and energy. This is true gorilla food. SERVES 4

¹/₂ cup seeded, soaked dates (see page 64), drained

4 to 6 bananas, peeled and thickly sliced (about 4 cups)

1 cup raw wheat germ

1 cup sprouted oats or buckwheat (see page 20)

In a food processor, blend all of the ingredients until well combined but still chunky. Form the mixture into small patties and place on a dehydrator tray. Using one of the methods described on page 28, dehydrate for 18 hours, flipping at least once during the drying time, and then serve.

Oat-Date Rawies

It's great to be able to make quick and tasty desserts. These simple treats keep well and are fabulous to break out when unexpected company stops in for a rawie and a glass of nut mylk. SERVES 4 TO 6

2 cups sprouted oats (see page 20)

1 cup seeded, soaked dates (see page 64), drained

1 cup soaked raisins (see page 64), drained

1 tablespoon ground cinnamon

Using a homogenizing juicer, homogenize the oats and dates until smooth and place in a large bowl. Stir in the raisins and cinnamon. For each rawie, form 2 tablespoons of the dough into a ball, place on a dehydrator tray, and press into a ¹/₂-inch round. Repeat for the remaining rawies. Using one of the methods described on page 28, dehydrate the rawies for 18 hours, or until dry, and then serve.

Sesame Rawies

These sweet little rawies are quick and easy to make and have a great crunch when fully dried. (Pictured opposite) SERVES 4 TO 6

2 cups sprouted sesame seeds (see page 20)

1 cup sunflower sprouts (see page 20)

1½ cups seeded, soaked dates (see page 64), drained

1 tablespoon pure vanilla extract

Pinch of black sesame seeds, for garnish

Using a homogenizing juicer, homogenize all of the ingredients until smooth and place in a large bowl. Form into ½-inch balls and place them on a dehydrator tray. Using one of the methods described on page 28, dehydrate the balls for about 12 hours, or until firm. Garnish with the sesame seeds, and then serve.

Carob-Hazelnut Torte

When I was visiting San Francisco in 1995, I helped this crazy cat Juliano start a restaurant called RAW. Eventually, I bought RAW and turned it into The Raw Experience, but before then, when RAW was being born, one of the first things I noticed was that Juliano had no desserts on the menu. I invented this torte and it became the first dessert served at RAW. Soon after, I was asked to print the recipe in the San Jose Mercury News. *I received hundreds of calls about it from people who loved it. This rich and filling treat became a standard at The Raw Experience.* SERVES 8 TO 12

2 cups seeded, soaked dates (see page 64), drained

3 cup soaked hazelnuts (see page 64), drained

1 cup raw carob powder

½ cup dried shredded coconut

2 tablespoons pure vanilla extract

2 cups Nut Crème (page 198)

1 cup Carob Sauce (page 207)

1 cup blackberries, for garnish

Mint leaves, for garnish

Using a homogenizing juicer, homogenize the dates and hazelnuts and place in a large bowl. Mix in the carob powder and coconut. Add the vanilla and mix. Using wet hands, roll the mixture into a ball. On a serving plate, press the ball into a flat circle, 1 inch thick. Top with the nut crème and drizzle with carob sauce. Garnish with the blackberries and mint leaves.

Bliss Balls

This recipe for these fantastic little treats is one of the oldest recipes I know. As a child, I learned to make nut-butter refrigerator balls. These Bliss Balls are the raw evolution of my mother's recipe. Many people tell me of the blissful experience they get from eating this most delectable of desserts. SERVES 4 TO 6

1 cup sprouted oats (see page 20) or Buckies (page 205)

1 cup seeded, soaked dates (see page 64), drained

1 cup raw nut butter (such as almond or hazelnut)

1/2 cup soaked raisins (see page 64), drained

1 teaspoon pure vanilla extract

1/4 cup raw carob powder

1 tablespoon ground cinnamon

1 cup raw wheat germ or sunflower seeds, ground into a fine powder (if needed to dry out mix)

1 cup sesame seeds

In a food processor, mix the oats, dates, nut butter, raisins, vanilla, carob, and cinnamon. Add the wheat germ only if the oat mixture is runny. The oat mixture should be tacky, like cookie dough. Spread the sesame seeds on a tray or plate. Roll the nut mixture into 1- to 2-inch balls, then roll the balls in the sesame seeds to coat and serve.

Cashew Sauce

This fabulous sauce is a smoother version of our standard nut crème. Use this one on any dessert, or just dip Fruit Rawies (page 102) in it. MAKES 2 CUPS

1 cup soaked cashews (see page 64), drained

4 seeded, soaked dates (see page 64), drained

1 teaspoon pure vanilla extract

1/4 cup filtered water

Combine all of the ingredients in a food processor or blender and blend until smooth.

Buckies

This recipe is one of the greatest ever invented. Buckies are a sprouted buckwheat snack treat, cereal, salad topping, and more. Their nutritional value is very high and the taste is delectable. This is possibly the crunchiest treat in the world of raw foods.
SERVES 4

2 cups dates, seeded

2 cups filtered water

1 teaspoon pure vanilla extract

4 cups sprouted buckwheat (see page 20), well drained

Place the dates in a bowl, cover with the water, and soak for about 1 hour, or until soft. Drain, reserving 1/2 cup of the liquid. Place the dates, reserved liquid, and vanilla in a blender and blend. Pour the date mixture into a large bowl, add the buckwheat sprouts, and mix well. Using one of the methods described on page 28, spread the mixture 1/2 inch thick on the appropriate drying surface and dehydrate the buckies for 7 to 10 hours. Crumble apart and use as a topping or just eat as a snack.

Ultimate Sundae

Something similar to this great dessert recipe came with my Champion Juicer. It is nice to know that the people who make this very versatile juicer enjoy the simplicity of raw ice cream. This dessert is a true winner. SERVES 2 TO 4

6 bananas, peeled, frozen, and thickly sliced

11 strawberries, frozen

2 cups fresh, finely chopped coconut meat (see page 50)

2 cups Cashew Sauce (page 204) or Carob Sauce (page 207)

Berries or chopped walnuts, for garnish

Using a homogenizing juicer with the blank plate in place, homogenize the bananas, strawberries, and coconut separately. Transfer equal amounts of each homogenized fruit to individual bowls. Stir the homogenized fruits in each bowl until swirled. Top each with some of the cashew sauce and berries, or carob sauce and crushed walnuts, and serve immediately.

Carrot Kake

This delicious dessert is as simple as can be. Carrot pulp (the part that is left when juice is removed) is a very versatile substance that is sweet, light, and easy to form. This recipe is a perfect way to make use of its many virtues. SERVES 8 TO 12

FROSTING

1¹/₂ cups soaked cashews (see page 20), drained

¹/₂ cup seeded, soaked dates (see page 64), drained

¹/₄ cup freshly squeezed lemon juice

1 tablespoon pure vanilla extract

3 cups sprouted almonds (see page 20)

2 cups seeded, soaked dates (see page 64), drained

2 cups soaked raisins (see page 64), drained

6 cups carrot pulp (from juicing carrots)

1 tablespoon freshly grated lemon zest

1 tablespoon freshly grated orange zest

1 tablespoon ground cinnamon

¹/₂ tablespoon freshly ground nutmeg

1 tablespoon ground cardamom

To prepare the frosting, place the cashews, dates, lemon juice, and vanilla in a blender and blend until smooth. Set aside.

To prepare the kake, using a homogenizing juicer, homogenize the almonds, dates, and raisins into a large bowl. Add the carrot pulp, lemon and orange zests, cinnamon, nutmeg, and cardamom, and mix well. On a serving plate, form into a cake shape and top with the frosting. Refrigerate until chilled before serving.

Six-Layer Carob Kake

This fabulous cake was originally created for a wedding. These cakes can turn out beautifully if you decorate and garnish them well, so be artistic. SERVES 10 TO 12

6 bananas

2 cups seeded, soaked dates (see page 64), drained

$^1/_2$ cup raw wheat germ

2 cups raw carob powder

1 cup sprouted walnuts (see page 20)

CAROB SAUCE

4 seeded, soaked dates (see page 64), drained

$^1/_4$ cup raw carob powder

2 tablespoons olive oil

3 cups Nut Crème (page 198)

Using a homogenizing juicer, homogenize the bananas, dates, wheat germ, carob, and walnuts into a bowl. Divide the dough into six equal-size balls and form six round, flat layers of similar width and diameter. Using one of the methods described on page 28, dehydrate the dough for 12 hours, or until dry.

To prepare the sauce, place the dates, carob powder, and olive oil in a blender cup or blender and blend well.

To assemble the cake, place one of the six layers on a plate. Spread $^1/_2$ cup of the nut crème over the layer. Continue layering, alternating cake and frosting, with the next five layers. Generously frost the top and sides of the cake. Drizzle with the carob sauce and serve.

Apple Kake

This ultimately healthy cake is a light and spicy dessert that lets you have your cake and eat it, too. SERVES 4 TO 6

1 cup flax seeds

1/2-inch piece fresh ginger

1 cup sprouted oats
(see page 20)

1 cup seeded, soaked dates
(see page 64), drained

1 teaspoon ground cinnamon,
plus additional for garnish

1 teaspoon freshly ground
nutmeg

1 tablespoon freshly grated
lemon zest

2 apples, peeled, cored, and
shredded (about 1 1/2 cups)

Nut Crème (page 198, optional)

In a spice grinder or blender cup, grind the flax seeds into a fine powder. Finely grate the ginger on a ginger grater or fine grater to extract the juice (you should have about 1 teaspoon). In a food processor, process the flax seed powder, ginger juice, oats, dates, cinnamon, nutmeg, and lemon zest until smooth. Transfer to a bowl and fold in the shredded apples. Form the mixture into a cake shape, 4 inches thick and 9 inches in diameter. Using one of the methods described on page 28, dehydrate the cake for 4 to 6 hours, until it has a dry outer layer and feels firm to the touch. Frost with the nut crème, sprinkle cinnamon on top to garnish, and allow to set in the refrigerator for about 2 hours before serving.

Reading List

Following is a list of some books about or relating to raw foods. Some of the titles are out of print, but you may be able to special order them via booksellers or find them in used-book stores.

Fruitarianism and Physical Rejuvenation
by O. L. M. Abramowski, MD

Light Eating for Survival
by Marcia Acciardo

Blatant Raw Foodist Propaganda
by Joe Alexander

Juel Anderson's Sea Green Primer: A Beginner's Book of Seaweed Cookery
by Juel Anderson

Nature's First Law
by Stephen Arlin, Fouad Dini, and David Wolfe

The Garden of Eden Raw Fruit and Vegetable Recipes
by Phyllis Avery

Books by Elizabeth Baker:
Un Cookbook
Gourmet Un Cookbook

Digestion, Assimilation, Elimination, and You
by Ed Bashaw and Michael Diogo

Books by Victoria Bidwell:
Get Well Recipes from the Garden of Eden
Simply Good

Eating Without Heating
by Sergei and Valya Boutenko

Books by Paul Bragg:
South Sea Culture of the Abdomen
Salt Free Health Sauerkraut Cookbook

Living Foods for Radiant Health
by Elaine Bruce

Regenerative Diet
by Dr. John R. Christopher, N.D., M. H.

Rejuvenation Diet
by Dr. J. Christopher

Living Foods for Optimum Health
by Brian Clement

Living Foods Lifestyle
by Brenda Cobb

Rainbow Green Live-Food Cuisine
by Gabriel Cousens

How to Dry Fruit
by Deanna DeLong

Living Foods
by George and Doris Fathman

The Raw Food Primer
by Suzanne Alex Ferrara

Feasting on Raw Foods
by Charles Gerras

Stalking the Wild Asparagus
by Euell Gibbons

Complete Nutritional Health Facts
by Health Research

The Secrets of Spirulina
by Christopher Hills

I Live on Fruit
by Essie Honiball and Terry C. Fry

Enzyme Nutrition
by Dr. Edward Howell

Eydie Mae's Natural Recipes
by Eydie Mae Hunsburger
and Chris Loeffler

Delights of the Garden
by Imar Hutchins

Books by Bernard Jensen:
The Real Soup and Salad Book
Blending Magic
The Healing Power of
   Chlorophyll

The LifeFood Recipe Book
by Annie and David Jubb

Sweet Temptations
by Frances Kendall

Live Food Juices
by H. E. Kirshner

Fruit the Food and Medicine
   for Man
by Morris Krok

Books by Viktoras Kulvinskas:
Survival into the 21st Century
Love Your Body
Sprout for the Love of
   Every Body
Life in the 21st Century

Vibrant Living
by James Levin, MD, and
Natalie Cederquist

Elaina's Pure Joy Kitchen
by Elaina Love

Dry It—You'll Like It
by Gen MacManiman

Wheatgrass Juice: Gift of
   Nature
by Betsy Russell Manning

Books by Elysa Markowitz:
Warming Up to Living Foods
Living with Green Power

Rawsome
by Brigitte Mars

Metaphysics of Raw Foods
by Stella McDermott

Books by Steve "the Sprout-
man" Meyerowitz:
Sproutman's Kitchen Garden
   Cookbook
Recipes from the Sproutman
Wheatgrass: Nature's Finest
   Medicine

Sprouts
by Esther Munroe

The Raw Life
by Paul Nison

Raw Food Treatment of
   Cancer
by Kristine Nolfi, MD

The Complete Book of Spices
by Jill Norman

Books by Frédéric Patenaude:
The Raw Secrets
Sunfood Cuisine

Hooked on Raw
by Rhio

Dining in the Raw
by Rita Romano

Herbs & Things
by Jeanne Rose

Soups Alive
by Eleanor Rosenast

Vital Creations
by Chad Sarno

Cereal Grass
by Ronald Seibold

Raw Gourmet
by Nomi Shannon

Angel Foods
by Cherie Soria

Raw Kids
by Cheryl Stoycoff

Books by Edmond Bordeaux
Szekely:
Essene Gospel of Peace
Scientific Vegetarianism
The Book of Living Foods
The Ecological Health Garden

Tropical Fruit
by Desmond Tate

Raw
by Charlie Trotter and
Roxanne Klein

Living Cuisine
by Renée Underkoffler

The Great Exotic Fruit Book
by Norman Van Aken

The Original Diet
by Karen Cross Whyte

Books by Dr. Ann Wigmore:
Be Your Own Doctor
The Wheatgrass Book
The Sprouting Book
The Healing Power Within
Heal Your Body
Recipes for a Longer Life
Naturama

The Complete Book of Raw
   Food
by various authors

Glossary

ACIDOPHILUS: A type of helpful bacteria used in digestion.

AMYLASE: A digestive enzyme found in saliva.

ASSIMILATION: The ability to receive nutrients.

BIOACTIVE: Food with its life force.

BIODYNAMIC: A way of organic farming.

BIOGENIC: Promoting life.

CHARGE: To induce an electrical current and store it.

COMPOST: The breakdown of organic materials.

CONVENTIONALLY GROWN: Grown with chemicals and pesticides.

CULTIVATED: Grown for the purpose of eating.

CULTURED: Food with healthy bacteria living on it.

DEHYDRATED: Food with water evaporated from it.

ELIMINATION: The expulsion of waste matter from the body.

ENEMA: A method of cleansing the colon using water.

ENZYME: Substance that splits food into its vital parts.

EVAPORATE: To remove water by using warmth.

EXFOLIATE: Stimulating the skin to release toxins.

FASTING: The removal of something from daily practice.

FECAL MUCOID MATTER: Old material stuck to the colon walls.

FORAGING: Finding wild food or questing for food.

FRUIT: Any water-rich food surrounding a seed.

GERMINATION: The beginning process of sprouting.

GRAIN: Any affixed hull seed that grows as a grass.

HERB: Any green plant whose leaves are edible.

HYBRID: Any food that has been bred.

INTENTION: The focus of positive energy toward a goal.

MACROBIOTIC: An Asian system of eating seasonal and mostly cooked foods.

NATURAL: Doing things in harmony with nature.

NUT: A seed that has a removable shell and grows on trees.

ORGANICALLY GROWN: Grown without the use of chemicals.

PAPAIN: A digestive enzyme found in papaya.

PREDIGESTED: Easier to assimilate due to living bacteria.

PREPARING: Creating a raw food meal.

REMINERALIZE: To introduce organic minerals to water.

SPROUT: The young growth of a future plant.

VEGAN: No animal products, meat, dairy, or eggs, and honey-free.

WILD: Produced by nature without any help from man.

WISDOM: Experience (what we do) plus knowledge (what we learn). A true understanding about some teachings that we can pass on to others to help benefit their life.

Index

algae, 34–35. *See also* spirulina
almonds, 45
  Almond-Corn Croquettes, 181
  Almond-Cumin Dressing, 146
  Almond Mylk, 70
  Almond-Onion-Parsley Soup, 126
  Apple-Almond Soup, 115
  Banalmond Bliss, 106
  Banalmond Mylk, 70
  Brownies, 197
  Carob Almond Crust, 198
  Carob Devastation, 196
  Carrot-Almond Essence
    Bread, 172
  Carrot-Almond Pâté, 164
  Carrot Kake, 206
  Cauliflower Chowder, 126
  Celery and Almond Butter, 91
  Cream of Broccoli Soup, 128
  Curried Almond Soup, 125
  Fruit and Nut Essence Bread, 172
  Lemon Bars, 200
  Nut Bliss, 80
  Nut Shake, 81
  Rosy Sea Soup, 118
  sprouting, 22, 126
  Sunny Red Pepper Pâté, 163
Aloe, Sweet Lime and, 80
Angel Hair with Marinara, 184
apples, 46, 57
  Apple-Almond Soup, 115
  Apple-Cinnamon Cup, 103
  Apple-Cinnamon Essence
    Bread, 171
  Apple Kake, 208
  Applesauce, 105
  Apples with Ginger Chutney, 100
  Apple Zing, 80
  Banaberry, 75
  Cinnamon-Apple Sprouted
    Wheat, 103
  Flaxative, 85
  Fruit Root, 75
  Intestinal Cleanse, 85
  Sunshine, 77
  Waldorf Salad, 132
  White Delight, 79
assimilation, 8–9

avocados, 47, 147
  Avocado-Parsley Dressing, 150
  Banacado, 75
  Creamy Herb Dressing, 147
  Rich and Creamy Seed Cheeze, 168
  Spirulina-Avocado Soup, 120
  Star Fruit Guacamole, 156
  Traditional Guacamole, 156

Baba Ghanoush, 174
bananas, 47
  Banaberry, 75
  Banacado, 75
  Banalmond Bliss, 106
  Banalmond Mylk, 70
  Banana Bread, 201
  Banana-Date Pudding, 108
  Banana Mylk, 71
  Complementary, 78
  Flaxative, 85
  Freedom's Froth, 78
  Green Dream, 72
  Mango Pudding, 107
  Nut Bliss, 80
  Nut-Free Crust, 198
  Nut Shake, 81
  Papaya Fundae, 109
  Six-Layer Carob Kake, 207
  Storange Smooth, 72
  Sunshine, 77
  Tangy Tango, 74
  Thin Mint, 83
  Tropical Ambrosia, 83
  Ultimate Sundae, 205
  White Delight, 79
Basic Seed Cheeze, 166
Basic Tofu, 93
beans, 36–37. *See also*
  garbanzo beans
beets, 39
  Borscht, 123
  Cashew-Beet Pâté, 162
  Iron Lion, 82
bell peppers, 42
  Chile Mole, 160
  Creamy Red Pepper Soup, 121
  Focaccia, 188
  Green Papaya Salad, 138

  Mexican Wild Rice and Tofu, 178
  Pineapple-Pepper Salad, 106
  Red Pepper–Chipotle Salsa, 158
  Sunny Red Pepper Pâté, 163
berries, 47–48. *See also individual*
  berries
  Banaberry, 75
  Berry Soup, 115
  Fennel-Berry Soup, 113
Black Raspberry Kreme, 109
Black Raspberry–Prickly Pear, 74
blenders, 61
Bliss Balls, 204
blueberries, 47
  Complementary, 78
  Fennel-Berry Soup, 113
  Persimmon Sunburst, 104
Borscht, 123
Bragg Liquid Aminos, 54, 57
bread
  Apple-Cinnamon Essence
    Bread, 171
  Banana Bread, 201
  Caraway-Onion Essence
    Bread, 173
  Carrot-Almond Essence Bread, 172
  Essence (Essene), 170
  Focaccia, 188
  Fruit and Nut Essence Bread, 172
  Herbed Essence Bread, 171
  Unstuffing, 165
broccoli, 40
  Cream of Broccoli Soup, 128
  Shangri La, 194
Brownies, 197
buckwheat, 43
  Banana Bread, 201
  Buckies, 205

cabbage, 40
  Borscht, 123
  Cabbage Rolls, 96
  Creamy Coleslaw, 141
  Kimchee, 154
  Sea Salad, 140
  Shangri La, 194
cacao, 48, 57

cakes
- Apple Kake, 208
- Carob Devastation, 196
- Carrot Kake, 206
- Six-Layer Carob Kake, 207

cantaloupe. *See* melons

Caraway-Onion Essence Bread, 173

carob, 48
- Bliss Balls, 204
- Brownies, 197
- Carob Almond Crust, 198
- Carob Devastation, 196
- Carob-Hazelnut Torte, 202
- Carob Sauce, 109, 207
- Frozen Fudge, 200
- Six-Layer Carob Kake, 207
- Thin Mint, 83

carrots, 39
- Carob Devastation, 196
- Carrot-Almond Essence Bread, 172
- Carrot-Almond Pâté, 164
- Carrot-Cashew-Ginger
  Dressing, 151
- Carrot Kake, 206
- Carrot–Pine Nut Dip, 91
- Corn, Carrot, and Pea Salad, 133
- Creamy Carrot-Ginger Soup, 118
- Creamy Coleslaw, 141
- Curried Almond Soup, 125
- Fruit Root, 75
- Iron Lion, 82
- Sunflower-Carrot Croquettes, 181
- Sweet Mustard Dressing, 147
- Tofu Loaf, 180

Cascadilla Soup, 121

cashews, 45
- Black Raspberry Kreme, 109
- Carrot-Cashew-Ginger
  Dressing, 151
- Carrot Kake, 206
- Cashew-Beet Pâté, 162
- Cashew Mylk, 71
- Cashew Sauce, 204
- Nectarine-Cardamom Soup, 112
- Pumpkin-Cashew Seed Cheeze, 167
- White Sauce, 95

cauliflower, 40
- Cauliflower Chowder, 126

celery, 39
- Celery and Almond Butter, 91
- Cooling Green, 86
- Green Clean, 77
- Waldorf Salad, 132

cherimoyas, 46
- Cherimoya Freeze, 105
- White Delight, 79

Chile Mole, 160

chiles, 41–42
- Fire Water, 81
- Red Pepper–Chipotle Salsa, 158

chlorophyll, 19

Cinnamon-Apple Sprouted
  Wheat, 103

coconut, 50–51, 58
- Carob Devastation, 196
- Carob-Hazelnut Torte, 202
- Coconut Custard, 199
- Coconut Milk, 77
- Corn Chips, 90
- Curry Sauce, 191
- Frozen Fudge, 200
- Nature's Nectar, 78
- Nut Bliss, 80
- Thin Mint, 83
- Tom Yum, 120
- Tropical Ambrosia, 83
- Ultimate Sundae, 205

Coleslaw, Creamy, 141

Colorful Tofu Salad, 169

Complementary, 78

condiments, 54–56

Cooling Green, 86

corn, 44
- Almond-Corn Croquettes, 181
- Chile Mole, 160
- Corn, Carrot, and Pea Salad, 133
- Corn Chips, 90
- Corn Chowder, 125
- Festive Sprouted Wild Rice, 179
- Tamales, 179

cranberries, 47
- Cranberry Sauce, 165

Cream of Broccoli Soup, 128

Cream of Zucchini Soup, 124

Creamy Carrot-Ginger Soup, 118

Creamy Coleslaw, 141

Creamy Herb Dressing, 147

Creamy Red Pepper Soup, 121

cucumbers, 57
- Cooling Green, 86
- Cucumber-Dill Dressing, 151
- Cucumber-Dill Soup, 124
- Cucumber-Jicama Salad, 133

cultured foods, 10, 21, 24–26, 62–63

Curried Almond Soup, 125

Curry, Thai, 191

Curry Sauce, 191

dates, 51
- Apple Kake, 208
- Banana-Date Pudding, 108
- Bliss Balls, 204
- Brownies, 197
- Buckies, 205
- Carob Devastation, 196
- Carob-Hazelnut Torte, 202
- Carrot Kake, 206
- Frozen Fudge, 200
- Lemon Bars, 200
- Oat-Date Rawies, 201
- Sesame Rawies, 202
- Six-Layer Carob Kake, 207
- soaking, 64

dehydrated foods, 10, 26–29, 63

Deluxe Salad, 134

dressings
- Almond-Cumin Dressing, 146
- Avocado-Parsley Dressing, 150
- Carrot-Cashew-Ginger
  Dressing, 151
- Creamy Herb Dressing, 147
- Cucumber-Dill Dressing, 151
- Green Goddess Dressing, 148
- Herbed Vinaigrette, 149
- Italian Dressing, 152
- Mango-Ginger Vinaigrette, 149
- Miso-Tahini Dressing, 148
- Peanut-Curry Dressing, 150
- Spicy Papaya-Lime Dressing, 152
- Sweet Mustard Dressing, 147
- Waldorf Salad Dressing, 146

drinks. *See also* mylk
- Apple Zing, 80
- Banaberry, 75
- Banacado, 75
- Black Raspberry–Prickly Pear, 74
- Coconut Milk, 77
- Complementary, 78
- Cooling Green, 86
- eVe-8, 86
- Fire Water, 81
- Flaxative, 85
- Freedom's Froth, 78
- Fruit Root, 75
- Ginger Blast, 82
- Green Clean, 77
- Green Dream, 72
- Intestinal Cleanse, 85
- Iron Lion, 82
- Lilistar, 82
- Liver Cleanse, 84
- Mellow Melon, 79
- Nature's Nectar, 78
- Nut Bliss, 80
- Nut Shake, 81
- Rejuvelac, 84
- Ruby Cooler (Sun Tea), 76
- Soursop-Pineapple, 83

drinks, continued
   Sprout Power, 76
   Storange Smooth, 72
   Sunshine, 77
   Sweet Lime and Aloe, 80
   Tangy Tango, 74
   Thin Mint, 83
   Tropical Ambrosia, 83
   White Delight, 79
dulse. *See* sea vegetables

eggplant, 41
   Baba Ghanoush, 174
   Lasagna, 185
elimination, 8–9
enzymes, 8
Essenes, 3, 170
eVe-8, 86
Exotic Fruit Salad, 98

Fabulous Fig Parfaits, 110
Falafel, 182
farmers' markets, 30
Fennel-Berry Soup, 113
Festive Seed Cheeze, 167
Festive Sprouted Wild Rice, 179
figs, 51
   Brownies, 197
   Fabulous Fig Parfaits, 110
Fire Water, 81
flax seeds, 44
   Almond-Corn Croquettes, 181
   Apple Kake, 208
   Flaxative, 85
   Flax-Dulse Chips, 90
   Herbed Essence Bread, 171
   Tamales, 179
flowers, edible, 32–33
   Mixed Field Greens with Edible
     Flowers, 130
   Ruby Cooler (Sun Tea), 76
Focaccia, 188
food. *See also* raw food
   bio-destructive to bio-genic, 14
   cultured, 10, 21, 24–26, 62–63
   dehydrated, 10, 26–29, 63
   fresh, 10, 15–18
   groups, four living, 10, 13
   local, 57
   organic, 7, 15, 56–57
   processed, 7
food combining, 15–16
food processors, 62
Freedom's Froth, 78
fresh foods, 10, 15–18

Frozen Fudge, 200
fruits, 46–54. *See also individual*
   fruits
Fudge, Frozen, 200

garbanzo beans, 36
   Falafel, 182
   Middle Eastern Plate, 182
   Sprouted Hummus, 174
gardening, indoor, 17
Garden Salad, 131
Garlic-Herb Oil, 188
garnishing, 62, 64–65
Gazpacho, 122
   Maui Onion Gazpacho, 123
ginger, 39
   Ginger Blast, 82
   Ginger-Pear Soup, 112
grains, 44–45
grapes, 54
   Waldorf Salad, 132
Greek Salad, 139
Green Clean, 77
Green Dream, 72
Green Goddess Dressing, 148
Green Papaya Salad, 138
greens, 37–38. *See also* salads
guacamole
   Star Fruit Guacamole, 156
   Traditional Guacamole, 156

hazelnuts, 45
   Carob-Hazelnut Torte, 202
herbs, 31–32
   Creamy Herb Dressing, 147
   dehydrating, 29
   Herbed Essence Bread, 171
   Herbed Garlic Seed Cheeze, 168
   Herbed Vinaigrette, 149
   Italian Dressing, 152
honey, 57
Hummus, Sprouted, 174

intention, 3, 6, 67
Intestinal Cleanse, 85
Iron Lion, 82
Italian Dressing, 152

jicama, 39
   Cucumber-Jicama Salad, 133
juicing, 16, 59–61

Kabobs, Veggie, 92
Kimchee, 154
kiwis, 52, 74
   Pineapple-Pepper Salad, 106
   Tangy Tango, 74

Lasagna, 185
legumes, 36–37. *See also* garbanzo
   beans; peanuts; peas
lemons, 49
   Lemon Bars, 200
lentils, 36
Lilistar, 82
limes, 49
   Spicy Papaya-Lime Dressing, 152
   Spicy Papaya-Lime Soup, 116
   Sweet Lime and Aloe, 80
Little Italy Salad, 137
Liver Cleanse, 84

macadamia nuts, 45
   White Sauce, 95
mangos, 52
   Complementary, 78
   Mango Bliss, 104
   Mango-Ginger Vinaigrette, 149
   Mango Pudding, 107
   Tribal Wild Rice Salad, 177
Maui Onion Gazpacho, 123
Mayonnaise, Raw, 146
melons, 42–43. *See also* watermelon
   Mellow Melon, 79
   Mixed Melon Ball Salad, 100
   Peach-Melon Soup, 114
Mexican Wild Rice and Tofu, 178
Middle Eastern Plate, 182
Mini Pizzas, 94
Miso-Tahini Dressing, 148
Mixed Field Greens with Edible
   Flowers, 130
Mixed Melon Ball Salad, 100
mole
   Chile Mole, 160
   Pea Mole, 161
mushrooms, 35–36
   Little Italy Salad, 137
Mustard Dressing, Sweet, 147
mylk
   Almond Mylk, 70
   Banalmond Mylk, 70
   Banana Mylk, 71
   Cashew Mylk, 71

Nature's Nectar, 78
Nectarine-Cardamom Soup, 112
nori. *See* sea vegetables
Nut-Free Crust, 198
nuts, 45, 58. *See also individual nuts*
   Nut Bliss, 80
   Nut Kreme, 110
   Nut Shake, 81
   soaking and sprouting, 22–23, 64
   Star Fruit and Raspberry-Nut
     Kreme, 102

oats, 44
   Apple Kake, 208
   Banana Bread, 201
   Bliss Balls, 204
   Lemon Bars, 200
   Oat-Date Rawies, 201
olives
   Greek Salad, 139
   Star Fruit Salsa, 157
   Tapenade, 169
   Tomatillo Salsa, 159
onions, 41
   Caraway-Onion Essence Bread, 173
   Maui Onion Gazpacho, 123
   Onion-Walnut Pâté, 161
oranges, 49–50
   Complementary, 78
   Fire Water, 81
   Liver Cleanse, 84
   Ruby Cooler (Sun Tea), 76
   Storange Smooth, 72
   Sweet Lime and Aloe, 80
organic foods, 7, 15, 56–57

papayas, 52
   Freedom's Froth, 78
   Green Dream, 72
   Green Papaya Salad, 138
   Papaya Fundae, 109
   Spicy Papaya-Lime Dressing, 152
   Spicy Papaya-Lime Soup, 116
   Tangy Tango, 74
passion fruit, 52
   Lilistar, 82
pâté
   Carrot-Almond Pâté, 164
   Cashew-Beet Pâté, 162
   Onion-Walnut Pâté, 161
   Sunny Red Pepper Pâté, 163
peaches
   Complementary, 78
   Peach-Melon Soup, 114
peanuts, 36
   Curry Sauce, 191
   Peanut-Curry Dressing, 150
pears, 53
   Ginger-Pear Soup, 112
peas, 36–37
   Corn, Carrot, and Pea Salad, 133
   Pea Mole, 161
   Pea Soup, 127
pecans, 45
   Nut Kreme, 110
   Praline Crust, 198
   Pumpkin Butter, 173

persimmons, 53
   Persimmon Soup, 115
   Persimmon Sunburst, 104
   Sunshine, 77
pesto
   Pesto Pizza, 186
   Pesto Soup, 127
   Pesto Wraps, 89
   Presto Pesto, 89
Pies, Raw Fruit, 198–99
pineapple, 53, 107
   Ginger Blast, 82
   Pineapple-Ginger Pudding, 107
   Pineapple-Pepper Salad, 106
   Soursop-Pineapple, 83
   Tropical Ambrosia, 83
   Veggie Kabobs, 92
pine nuts, 45
   Carrot–Pine Nut Dip, 91
   Seven-Star Sauce, 194
pizzas
   Mini Pizzas, 94
   Pesto Pizza, 186
   Pizza Crusts, 94, 187
   Traditional Pizza, 186
Praline Crust, 198
Presto Pesto, 89
prickly pears, 53, 74
   Black Raspberry–Prickly Pear, 74
processed foods, 7
puddings
   Banana-Date Pudding, 108
   Mango Pudding, 107
   Pineapple-Ginger Pudding, 107
pumpkin, 43
   Pumpkin Butter, 173
   Pumpkin-Cashew Seed Cheeze, 167

quinoa, 44
   Rejuvelac, 84
   Tabouli, 144

raspberries, 47, 48
   Banaberry, 75
   Black Raspberry Kreme, 109
   Black Raspberry–Prickly Pear, 74
   Fennel-Berry Soup, 113
   Raspberry Sauce, 110
   Star Fruit and Raspberry-Nut Kreme, 102
   Tangy Tango, 74
raw food
   advocates of, 3–4
   balanced diet of, 11
   benefits of, 5, 6
   finding, 30, 65–66
   principles of, 1–3

transitioning to, 2, 11–13
   travel and, 27, 66–67
Raw Fruit Pies, 198–99
Raw Mayonnaise, 146
Red Pepper–Chipotle Salsa, 158
Red Sauce, 95
Rejuvelac, 84
rice, 44–45
Rich and Creamy Seed Cheeze, 168
Root Slaw, 142
Rosy Sea Soup, 118
Ruby Cooler (Sun Tea), 76

salads. See also dressings
   Colorful Tofu Salad, 169
   Corn, Carrot, and Pea Salad, 133
   Creamy Coleslaw, 141
   Cucumber-Jicama Salad, 133
   Deluxe Salad, 134
   Exotic Fruit Salad, 98
   Garden Salad, 131
   Greek Salad, 139
   Green Papaya Salad, 138
   Little Italy Salad, 137
   Mixed Field Greens with Edible Flowers, 130
   Mixed Melon Ball Salad, 100
   Pineapple-Pepper Salad, 106
   Root Slaw, 142
   Sea Salad, 140
   Shredded Salad, 130
   Sprout Salad, 135
   Tabouli, 144
   Tribal Wild Rice Salad, 177
   Tropical Fruit Salad, 99
   Waldorf Salad, 132
   Zucchini-Squash Salad, 131
salsas
   Red Pepper–Chipotle Salsa, 158
   Star Fruit Salsa, 157
   Tomatillo Salsa, 159
sapotes, 53–54
   White Delight, 79
sea vegetables, 33–34
   dehydrating, 29
   Flax-Dulse Chips, 90
   Nori Rolls, 193
   Rosy Sea Soup, 118
   Sea Salad, 140
seeds, 43–44. See also individual seeds
   Basic Seed Cheeze, 166
   Festive Seed Cheeze, 167
   Herbed Garlic Seed Cheeze, 168
   Pumpkin-Cashew Seed Cheeze, 167
   Rich and Creamy Seed Cheeze, 168
   soaking and sprouting, 22–23, 64

sesame seeds, 44
  Bliss Balls, 204
  Sesame Rawies, 202
Seven-Star Sauce, 194
Shangri La, 194
Shredded Salad, 130
Six-Layer Carob Kake, 207
soups
  Almond-Onion-Parsley Soup, 126
  Apple-Almond Soup, 115
  Berry Soup, 115
  Borscht, 123
  Cascadilla Soup, 121
  Cauliflower Chowder, 126
  Corn Chowder, 125
  Cream of Broccoli Soup, 128
  Cream of Zucchini Soup, 124
  Creamy Carrot-Ginger Soup, 118
  Creamy Red Pepper Soup, 121
  Cucumber-Dill Soup, 124
  Curried Almond Soup, 125
  Fennel-Berry Soup, 113
  Gazpacho, 122
  Ginger-Pear Soup, 112
  Maui Onion Gazpacho, 123
  Nectarine-Cardamom Soup, 112
  Peach-Melon Soup, 114
  Pea Soup, 127
  Persimmon Soup, 115
  Pesto Soup, 127
  Rosy Sea Soup, 118
  Spicy Papaya-Lime Soup, 116
  Spirulina-Avocado Soup, 120
  Sweet Potato Soup, 128
  Tom Yum, 120
  Tropical Fruit Soup, 116
  Watermelon Soup, 113
soursop, 46
  Soursop-Pineapple, 83
Spicy Papaya-Lime Dressing, 152
Spicy Papaya-Lime Soup, 116
spirulina, 35, 58
  Green Dream, 72
  Spirulina-Avocado Soup, 120
sprouts, 10, 18–21, 22–23. See also
    individual seeds
  Sprouted Hummus, 174
  Sprout Power, 76
  Sprout Salad, 135
  tools for, 61–62
squash, 42, 43. See also pumpkin;
    zucchini
  Angel Hair with Marinara, 184
  Zucchini-Squash Salad, 131

star fruits
  Lilistar, 82
  Star Fruit and Raspberry-Nut
    Kreme, 102
  Star Fruit Guacamole, 156
  Star Fruit Salsa, 157
strawberries, 48
  Banaberry, 75
  Storange Smooth, 72
sunflower seeds, 44
  Almond-Corn Croquettes, 181
  Bliss Balls, 204
  Carob Devastation, 196
  Cucumber-Dill Soup, 124
  Green Goddess Dressing, 148
  Nori Rolls, 193
  Sesame Rawies, 202
  Sunflower-Carrot Croquettes, 181
  Sunny Red Pepper Pâté, 163
Sunshine, 77
Sun Tea (Ruby Cooler), 76
Sweet Lime and Aloe, 80
Sweet Mustard Dressing, 147
sweet potatoes, 40
  Sweet Potato Soup, 128

Tabouli, 144
Tamales, 179
Tangy Tango, 74
Tapenade, 169
Thai Curry, 191
Thin Mint, 83
tofu, 93
  Basic Tofu, 93
  Colorful Tofu Salad, 169
  Mexican Wild Rice and Tofu, 178
  Tamales, 179
  Tofu Loaf, 180
  Tofu-Stuffed Cherry Tomatoes, 93
tomatillos, 48, 159
  Tomatillo Salsa, 159
tomatoes, 42
  Angel Hair with Marinara, 184
  Cascadilla Soup, 121
  Chile Mole, 160
  Focaccia, 188
  Gazpacho, 122
  Little Italy Salad, 137
  Maui Onion Gazpacho, 123
  Pesto Soup, 127
  Red Sauce, 95
  Sprout Power, 76
  Tapenade, 169
  Tofu-Stuffed Cherry Tomatoes, 93

Tom Yum, 120
tools, 59–63
Torte, Carob-Hazelnut, 202
Traditional Guacamole, 156
Traditional Pizza, 186
Tribal Wild Rice Salad, 177
Tropical Ambrosia, 83
Tropical Fruit Salad, 99
Tropical Fruit Soup, 116

Ultimate Sundae, 205
Unstuffing, 165

Waldorf Salad, 132
Waldorf Salad Dressing, 146
walnuts, 45
  Apple-Cinnamon Essence
    Bread, 171
  Carob Devastation, 196
  Lasagna, 185
  Onion-Walnut Pâté, 161
  Presto Pesto, 89
  Six-Layer Carob Kake, 207
  Waldorf Salad, 132
  Walnut Zing Crust, 198
water, 9–10
watermelon, 43
  juicing, 79
  Mellow Melon, 79
  Mixed Melon Ball Salad, 100
  Watermelon Soup, 113
wheat, 45
  Cinnamon-Apple Sprouted
    Wheat, 103
  -grass, 20
  Pizza Crusts, 187
  Rejuvelac, 84
White Delight, 79
White Sauce, 95
wild rice, 44
  Festive Sprouted Wild Rice, 179
  Mexican Wild Rice and Tofu, 178
  Tamales, 179
  Tribal Wild Rice Salad, 177

yeast, nutritional, 55, 58

zucchini, 43
  Angel Hair with Marinara, 184
  Cream of Zucchini Soup, 124
  Lasagna, 185
  Pesto Wraps, 89
  Zucchini-Squash Salad, 131